T0361025

THE HEADTEACHER AS EFFECTIVE LEADER

To Gerry Clarke, an inspiring headteacher and leader
and Trudy Boyle, a follower of Lao-Tse

The Headteacher as Effective Leader

Bill Boyle
Paul Clarke

Routledge
Taylor & Francis Group

LONDON AND NEW YORK

First published 1998 by Ashgate Publishing

Reissued 2018 by Routledge
2 Park Square, Milton Park, Abingdon, Oxon, OX14 4RN
711 Third Avenue, New York, NY 10017, USA

Routledge is an imprint of the Taylor & Francis Group, an informa business

Publisher's Note
The publisher has gone to great lengths to ensure the quality of this reprint but points out that some imperfections in the original copies may be apparent.

Disclaimer
The publisher has made every effort to trace copyright holders and welcomes correspondence from those they have been unable to contact.

A Library of Congress record exists under LC control number: 97004411

ISBN 13: 978-1-138-34432-7 (hbk)
ISBN 13: 978-0-429-43858-5 (ebk)

Contents

List of figures

Introduction

A leader is best
When people barely know that he exists,
Not so good when people obey and acclaim him,
Worst when they despise him ...
But of a good leader, who talks little,
When his work is done, his aim fulfilled,
They will all say, 'We did this ourselves.'
Lao-tse

The learning community is 'a place where people continually expand their capacity to create the results they truly desire, where new and expansive patterns of thinking are nurtured, where collective aspiration is set free, and where people are continually learning how to learn together' (Senge, 1990).

How might a headteacher deal with the task of effectively leading a school in times of considerable change? This is an interesting question because many of the tasks that a headteacher does have little to do with change and everything to do with stability. Some of the changes that the headteacher might be expected to carry out are incomprehensible in educational terms, and yet headteachers are expected to lead in these areas. A book that intends to explore the change process through the lens of the headteacher and the leading role that the headteacher might take could be considered overambitious in the current context of school reform. Many innovations derive from outside the school gates and are optimistically expected to be in place in difficult if not impossible, time-scales. It is little wonder that headteachers see themselves as managers more than leaders, and frequently managers of the status quo rather than managers and leaders of a changing organisation.

Leaders are often required to do those things that many people find daunting. Senge (1990) describes a learning organisation using many of those words and images that leaders draw upon to engage and enthuse colleagues into action. The imagery and language used in the quote to describe a learning organisation, however, is perhaps quite different from those metaphors used to describe the current climate of schools. We often hear of the school 'struggling' to accommodate the required reforms, and 'battling' to maintain numbers, and 'scratching around' for resources. Such language says a lot about how our schools operate as organisations, how we go about establishing procedures and making and taking decisions inside this way of thinking.

Such combative terminology is often driven by what is described as 'top-down' management. This approach frequently functions by fragmenting the school into compartments, each of which is then analysed to make sense of its component parts, and delegated to a member of staff to deal with. We hear of line management, of accountability routes and areas of responsibility. These frameworks serve to provide a shape and in turn establish an internal meaning to the school. The meaning is therefore available to staff, and depending upon how well they all adhere to the shape, the system operates.

Were a school to be so simple and so simplistically possible to model and run! In a linear, rational and perhaps people-free world such a management approach would no doubt flourish. But the world that schools occupy is a world of messiness as well as clarity, of profound complexity, of numerous and often contradictory pressures, a world in which teachers still have sole custody of and the requirement to educate and nurture young minds on their future role in society.

Let us for a moment return to Senge's description of the learning organisation. He uses concepts such as expanding capacity, creating results that are desired, nurturing thinking and new ideas, aspiring collectively and learning together. All of these images of an organisation present a quite startling notion of those people who embody the organisation, having the power to make of it what they want.

The ways in which such an organisation is created are not impossible, wish-fulfilling dreams; they are built upon practical, people-centred strategies and processes that centre on:

- how decisions are made,
- how different systems are interlocked,
- how new ideas are facilitated,
- how priorities are established,
- how people understand each other's needs as well as those that they have themselves.

It has been suggested that these practices can be thought of in terms of two basic concepts: the first addresses people and interpersonal relationships, the second concerns that of production and task achievement (Blake and Moulton, 1984). This has recently been further developed to give a more dynamic representation of the role of leader addressing four frames for understanding organisations (Bolman and Deal, 1991):

- structural,
- human resource,
- political,
- and symbolic frames.

In the context of a school, Sergiovanni (1984) notes five leadership forces that explain how the performance of a leader is related to the performance of an excellent school:

- technical leadership – the way things get done,
- human leadership – assisting people to succeed,
- educational leadership – the head 'teacher',
- symbolic leadership – leading by example,
- cultural leadership – creating a climate for success.

Much of the research literature describes these various types of leadership, and advocates them as the routes to be taken for establishing a successful school. However, a limitation of much of the literature is the lack of any clear practical strategies that can facilitate, for example, a successful educational leadership role in school.

Using these concepts in this book, our aim is to be able to provide you with some of the routes that you might wish to explore with colleagues to create just such schools. We will examine each area and facet of the five types with reference to material that has been tried and tested in schools as they come to respond to change.

We particularly wish to focus attention on the sequence that we have selected for the chapters. The sequence is designed to follow a route that we have found successful; it does not prescribe this route, but it is presented in this way to prompt new ways of looking at some, probably quite familiar, concepts and activities.

The book therefore attempts to make sense of the central role that the effective headteacher plays in the development of a successful and adaptive school. The headteacher is in our view a crucial player in the development of an appropriate internal school climate. The leadership role demands the ability to engage strategically with complex and frequently changing needs and to encourage all staff to play their part in shaping school to meet with such demands. The mind-set that established the school system as one that could effectively run on mechanistic and technical and rational models of development no longer holds in schools that face forward into the next millennium. In this book we hope to provide you with strategies that can clearly and effectively enable you and your staff to explore the territory of organisational development for the next century where change will be continuous and complex. This book will begin the journey that examines how we can facilitate for headteachers and staff the leadership skills that effectively deal with today's management issues and can assist in the transformation of schools into their future organisational frames.

1 Audit: a point of view

How does our school 'think'? What are the approaches that it takes to the developmental work it undertakes, and what impact are these efforts having? Is it realistic to assume that we can in fact 'measure' improvement in any useful way?

This chapter will explore some of the territory which such questions raise. It is our intention to do two things: first, to raise some important questions about the ways in which we might usefully think about school improvement, and second, to offer some approaches that apply the thinking in the context of school development.

Intention to action – to review the audit process

An audit is a fascinating conceptual tool. It is often thought to be a device which is used to establish a base position, but it can operate in almost any situation at any point to provide a marker of the impact of a change. It can also be used to make sense of the underlying thinking that a school might be displaying, thereby providing valuable new information on the process of improvement taking place in a school.

An audit is rather like a commitment to action: we undertake one because there is a desire to investigate areas of the school that require greater amounts of information and data.

Having obtained data of various sorts (statistical, discussion, plans, reports etc) we then are faced with the issue of what such data mean and how that meaning is subsequently translated into action. This is an intervention problem: what do we understand our school data to mean? How can we best interpret it? And how will our interpretation be translated into actions? As these actions begin to happen during the school year we then begin to ask about the impact of the planned interventions and this might renew the auditing process. An audit is therefore a part of a larger process that links intention to action with review.

An audit process should be planned to flow from one set of activities to another. At the same time, an audit needs to be seen as part of a greater process of activity in school. It involves us in taking on a set of activities that move us personally and organisationally towards a more complex and interconnected series of operations that attempt to place a sense of greater order on a received situation. It can be isolated in a set of particular focal areas, but there is no doubt that the aftereffects of the audit will be significant and will spread into other, unsuspecting, areas of school life. This interconnected nature of audit to other factors in school means that we should not undertake an audit lightly, because in doing so we are drawing attention to details of the organisation that we live with but often leave aside in the day-to-day functioning of school.

If we were to liken the school to an organism, we might be awakening it from a period of hibernation and in waking it we do not necessarily know what we are going to discover, how ready it is for response and activity. Equally appropriate is the journey metaphor (Hopkins, Ainscow and West, 1994). The auditing process reveals the preparedness for the journey and creates a state of readiness and heightened awareness amongst individual staff and the organisation collectively.

Who should do the audit?

There are obviously going to be aspects of the audit that are beyond the scope of any one person. Indeed, it is not really desirable that one person in isolation should undertake the audit anyway. An effective audit should involve all those who are likely to be affected by the process. In doing so the headteacher is making a statement about the process of working that is in itself bigger than the task. It is implying that people have a role, a voice in the activity of the school, and that their voice will help to influence and inform the future direction of the school. The audit is therefore an important device for initiating other actions in school. Such actions will be the themes of other chapters of this book.

An audit is both objective and subjective. It demands that we stand back from the day-to-day routine and draw together information related to the issue under question; it also asks of us that we engage and ultimately select particular meaning from the information that we gather. The process is therefore complex in a social sense because people will convey and interpret different meaning from the data, and in a political sense because people will have their own desires and motivations to make particular selections. Audit is therefore a contested and contesting process: it should engage people. The danger is that the audit is made into a mechanical analysis of the school, attempting to construct a complete picture of what is happening. This is an impossible task because the picture will never be complete. It is far better to undertake an audit recognising that it will raise problems and new questions, and that with careful analysis it should facilitate deeper levels of thinking about the nature and methods of school as it goes about its activity.

Why are we going to do the audit?

This is a vital starting question. It is important to think about the reasons why you feel that this is a time that would benefit from an audit. It may be that you want to use the exercise to identify where to place most emphasis for the following year of staff development, it may be that there are particular concerns that you wish to address related to LEA or OFSTED reported findings that need to be undertaken. It might be that a group of staff have raised a need for a particular curriculum area to be revisited and developed.

Furthermore, it is likely that people will interpret the reason for the audit from different starting points. This is both useful, as it can be used as a method of widening staff involvement in the development of the school, and paradoxically difficult, because it means that time has to be spent initially making it clear what is going to happen, how it will happen and why it is happening in the way it is.

To move into an audit without exploring with staff the function of the exercise is courting disaster from the start. It is vital that the audit is an engaging process for all involved. As the first part of our approach to the process we are going to address some simple questions that in turn address the process of the audit.

Starting points

- What do you see as the most important reason for undertaking the audit?
- How will this be of use?
- What will you need to focus upon to achieve your goal/s?

Ongoing

- You will gather a great deal of information as you proceed to analyse the functioning of the school and your role and that of colleagues. How will you classify the information?

- What time-scale will you work to?
- How will data be reported back to yourself, senior management, and the whole team?

Completion

- What will you hope to produce having completed the audit?
- How will it need to look?
- What will show this?

Often these questions are better suited to groups of staff rather than being addressed in isolation. One simple procedure that you can adopt to gather ideas on how the audit might proceed and how it might be supported and successfully completed is to do the thinking individually, then pair up with colleagues, then share with the whole staff. This think–pair–share process is a powerful technique that facilitates team and personal growth on professional issues.

Further questions that relate to the end-goals

- Are there particular aspects of school operations that are difficult to visualise?
- Do you find that there really does not seem to be a clear agenda or idea of what you are moving into?
- Why do you think this is so?
- Is it because you personally are not sure of the directions that the school is moving in?
- Or is it a team issue?

Try to identify what is causing the lack of clarity of purpose.

It is important to have some clarity for the organisation and for individuals. Csikszentmihalyi (1992) identifies four vital components that are central to a sense of flow in self and organisation which facilitates a feeling of purpose and well-being that can permeate successful development of self and school.

The four components are:

1. Setting goals: This demonstrates the ability to make choices ranging from the trivial to the significant. The selection of a goal is related to the recognition of challenges. We need to develop our ability to identify those key challenges that exist in the school and then be able to articulate them clearly to our colleagues.
2. Becoming immersed in the activity: After deciding on a course of action

there is a need to become immersed in the activity. This means investing attention in the task in hand. There is a balance between the opportunities for taking action and the skills that one might possess for carrying out such actions. The underlying factor here is that it is imperative that one is aware of the possibility of the goals, and that one knows one's own limitations and strengths. If a goal is excessively unrealistic, then it is less likely it will be reached. There is therefore a need to balance the demands of the goal and the environment in which it is being carried out with the people and skills that are available to realise the goal.

Attention to the task is a central aspect of becoming immersed in the activity. This implies that we are not distracted from the goal by a myriad of other conflicting issues.

3. Paying attention to what is happening: Increased concentration on the task then leads to an increase of involvement which can only be maintained if there are frequent and focused bursts of attention to the goal. In a complex set of changes, the need to remain tuned in to what is taking place is essential, otherwise the sustained involvement needed will lapse.

4. Learning to enjoy the immediate experience: The outcome, according to Csikszentmihalyi, of learning to set goals, develop skills, be sensitive to feedback, to know how to concentrate and get involved (ibid., p.212) is that when times get hard, or difficult and tough, one can still maintain a sense of purpose and control. The living of the experience, and the attention to the slow progress through it enables the whole effect to be more powerful and fulfilling. People feel better when they are involved. The implication therefore is that they are encouraged and incorporated into the changes so that they too feel the changes taking place.

Flow drives individuals to creativity and outstanding achievement. The necessity to develop increasingly refined skills to sustain enjoyment is what lies behind the evolution of culture. It motivates both individuals and cultures to change into more complex entities (ibid., p. 212).

The audit skills that facilitate effective leading

*   Identification of key issues from a diverse range of data.
*   Paying attention to what is *and is not* happening.
*   Being sensitive to areas of weakness and strength and addressing the need realistically.
*   Staying focused, even when other demands press in on the direction and pace of the action.
*   Living the day-to-day experience and sharing the small successes and

insights. Don't be afraid that there are no major revelations.

This section has described a process of audit that raises questions about the application of and thinking about change in school. We have described the stages that are known to be important if one is to experience maximum enjoyment from the process of change. This might appear bizarre, to describe a process and how one might go about enjoying change. But we believe that it is a vital and frequently ignored element in the success of school change and it is a critical component in the repertoire of skill that the headteacher must prepare for and lead staff through.

Some useful focal areas for an audit to consider

Although the list of what one might audit is as long as the school might wish to consider, there are some central features of school life which will probably form part of the remit of an audit process. These are presented here in the form of a series of different headings adapted from the work of Danielson (1996).

ONE: Curriculum and planning

- Curriculum content and pedagogic knowledge

  - Are the staff informed in the content of the curriculum that they are teaching?
  - Are the staff confident of the links between different aspects of the curriculum they teach?
  - What is the range of teaching approaches used to instruct students in the curriculum content?
  - How effective is that range of approaches in achieving high pupil outcome performance?

- Knowledge of students' learning

  - Do staff demonstrate a knowledge of the characteristics of the age group they are teaching?
  - Is there a sensitivity to the diversity of student learning needs?
  - Do staff know the ways their students preferentially learn?
  - Is there an interest in the cultural background of the students?

- Teaching

  - Are there sufficient teaching resources available for staff to teach?
  - Are there sufficient resources available for students to learn?

- Learning approaches

    - How proficiently are learning activities constructed?
    - What use is made of materials and resources?
    - How are groups established?
    - How does the single lesson fit into the coherence of the wider curriculum?

- Students' learning

    - Are students assessed against teaching goals?
    - How are assessments used to inform planning?

TWO: The learning classroom

- The environment

    - How successfully does the teacher work with the students and establish a passionate learning climate?
    - How do students interact?

- A learning culture

    - How important is the content?
    - Are students proud of their work?
    - Are the expectations maintained at a high level?

- Classroom management

    - How are groups managed?
    - How are changes in the school day from lesson to lesson managed?
    - Are resources used with care and consideration?
    - How do non-professional staff work in class?

- Management of students

    - Are there clearly defined expectations?
    - Is student behaviour monitored?
    - What are the responses to inappropriate behaviour? Are they consistently applied?

- The use of space in the classroom

    - Is the furniture well laid out and safe?
    - Does the layout facilitate or inhibit learning?
    - Are resources accessible for all learners?

THREE: Teaching

- Communicating

- Are directions and procedures well defined and understood?
- Is spoken and written language clear?

- Talk

  - What is the quality of the questioning?
  - How are discussions facilitated and do these techniques work successfully for the context of the lessons?
  - Are all students engaged and participating?

- Involving students in learning

  - Do they have appropriate work?
  - Is the pace and structure of the work relevant?

- Feedback

  - What is the feedback like? Is it accurate? Constructive? Specific?
  - Are the students given sufficient time to do the work?

- Flexibility and responsiveness

  - Are the lessons modified according to need?
  - How sensitive is the response to student needs?
  - How persistent is the response to need?

FOUR: Professional duties

- Critical analysis of teaching

  - How accurate is the teacher's analysis of the success of the work?
  - How are the analyses applied to future activity?

- Maintenance of accurate records

  - Is there a record of work completed?
  - Do students reflect upon all activities that they are involved in?
  - How well is progress monitored?
  - Are these records used in planning?

- Communication with family

  - How successfully is the curriculum conveyed to the parents?
  - Is there high quality information provided on individual pupil performance?
  - Are families involved in the learning with students?

- School and local developments

  - Are there good staff relationships?

- – Are people committed to the school and to learning?
- – Are staff involved in their own learning?
- – Do staff attend relevant external courses and feed back to staff in school?

- ● Professionalism

  - – Are staff self-motivating?
  - – Are staff making their own decisions?
  - – Do staff lead?

There will be many further areas of school life that you can develop in the audit process. We have selected these because they have a central impact on the thinking about the teaching and learning taking place in the school.

Establishing the leader: what kind of leader am I?

We are now going to address some questions that refer to the type of leader that you might be in situations you experience in a school.

First, we want you to reflect on the following leads of sentences and to note down at least four lines on each of the leads. Think clearly and concisely about each one.

1. When I am confronted with rules ...
2. If somebody criticises me or my ideas ...
3. If someone clearly does not agree with me ...
4. If I am uncertain about an issue ...
5. When someone tells me what to do ...

Look at your responses and determine the following:

1. Are your responses impulsive, reflecting concern about yourself?
2. Are your responses concerned with behaving in socially acceptable ways, evaluating situations in simple concrete terms, and sensitive to figures of authority?
3. Are your responses indicative of being open to the ideas of others and able to evaluate alternatives? Do they show an increased tolerance for uncertainty and a need for independence?
4. Do your responses suggest that you weigh up alternatives before deciding on best solutions to problems, show a concern for the consequences of decisions and are secure and independent?

We are going to use this as a springboard to examine more deeply the type of leadership you apply to different situations. It does not assume that there is one, single form of leadership that is taken on and adhered to in all circumstances.

In each of the following six areas of leadership we want you to identify your five main strengths and weaknesses.

1. Technical leadership: the ways in which I establish and maintain structural changes to policy, procedures etc.

Technical leadership	Strengths	Weaknesses

2. Human leadership: the ways in which I manage people and enable them to excel and realise their potential.

Human leadership	Strengths	Weaknesses

3. Educational leadership: the ways in which I can work as a lead professional in the teaching and learning activity of the school.

Educational leadership	Strengths	Weaknesses

4. Symbolic leadership: the way in which I facilitate leadership in my actions.

Symbolic leadership	Strengths	Weaknesses

5. Cultural leadership: The way in which I establish and manage a climate that represents the purpose, values, attitudes and beliefs of those people involved in the day-to-day life of the school.

Cultural leadership	Strengths	Weaknesses

6. Transformational leadership: The way in which I successfully enable the school and those staff and students within to develop and be creative in their dealing with transformations of the school from one activity to another.

Transformational leadership	Strengths	Weaknesses

Interpretation of the tables

Try to be specific about what types of situation these components operate in. You have by now developed some areas of personal strengths and weaknesses in line with the leadership role. You are now in a position to reflect a little on these roles, and to address the implications of the information you have placed in the tables.

What does this tell you of your personal view of your style of leadership?

Do you have a skewed profile: i.e. one that strongly moves in one direction against one or more of the attributes listed?

Other issues to consider

- Does circumstance determine my style of leadership?
- Or is it the case that I will not be thrown off course by circumstance?

Some recent research described by Blase and Anderson (1996) presents in the form of a matrix four leadership styles that reflect the micropolitical nature of the role, that is, the ways in which a leader assumes or displays power in different situations in which a leadership role is necessary (see Figure 1.1).

The intention here is not to assume that any one of these roles is always evident. Rather, we are interested in using the matrix as a device that allows us to reflect upon the ways that different situations facilitate or sometimes impose particular styles of leadership response.

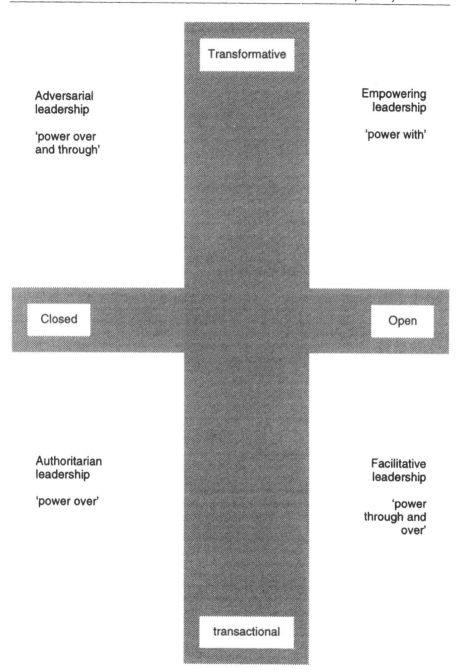

Figure 1.1   Micropolitical leadership matrix
Source: Blase and Anderson, 1995, p.18.

Issues in which your style of leadership might be affected

1. A meeting with staff at the start of the term establishes an outcome which means that three members of staff are in favour of adopting a new planning procedure and three are against. What style of response will you take in the impasse?
2. You and the teaching staff are keen to adopt a peer tutoring scheme, but a strong minority of the parents are fervently against it.
3. A first meeting with your staff following your appointment as the new headteacher.
4. Assembly with the whole school following a serious act of vandalism.

Now carry out the following exercise:

-   Record your responses to each situation below: note which style you think/know you would adopt.
-   Note down the reasons.
-   Record how you might address the issue were you to adopt an approach that reflects a different leadership style. What might you say or do in that situation?

What does this teach you about the strengths and weaknesses of your preferred style of approach?

My philosophy: finding out about the things that matter to me in my role as headteacher

What matters to me most about this school? Often the opportunity to stop and reflect upon what it is that makes one personally feel good about the job is left aside while one deals with more pressing, immediate needs. However, it is quite apparent that schools that are effectively led do have a sense of individual and collective purpose. This section aims to provide some simple starting questions to be explored.

We suggest that the question is asked, and then revisited each day if possible for a period of about one week. During that period you will have had an opportunity to live the day-to-day life of your school, but you will also be in a position to reflect on those parts of the work that matter most to you. There are no 'right' answers to this; the intention is to create some reflective space, and to initiate a series of lines of inquiry that can develop your skills leading towards an effective analysis of school needs.

We would like you to make a list of the issues, feelings, approaches, places, procedures, people, relationships that mean most to you in your school. Try to spend about ten minutes each day for a week reflecting on and adding to this list, using the Personal Diary in Figure 1.2.

At the end of the week take a careful look at the list you have established and try to classify the responses to the question into the dimensions of school activity, using the format shown in Figure 1.3.

Following five days of notes and then some clarification and synthesis of what has been noted, you now have a table of elements of school life that matter a good deal to you. To what extent does this table cross-reference with the one that you established on an identification of your strengths and weaknesses?

- Do you find that there is a close correlation between what you like about school life and what you believe to be your personal strengths? If so, what conclusions can you draw from the findings? If not, then what conclusions can you draw from the findings?
- Are you finding that your responses follow a particular set of dimensions? Are you finding that some of these dimensions really don't register as much or at all?
- To what extent do you see the 'gaps' in the dimensions as being an indication of a wider 'need' within school? Where would you go for evidence to support your insights?

Your perspective of what matters

Now take a closer look at the responses in the dimensions that are well supported. This is representative of your perspective on what matters in school. It can be interpreted as a representation of those aspects of the role of leader that you will be seen to take most time for, and care to nurture and develop. In what ways do the following groups of people in the school experience your attachment of importance to these dimensions of school life?

1. To teaching colleagues?

2. To pupils?

3. To parents?

4. To the wider community?

5. To school visitors?

6. To school governors?

DAY ONE

DAY TWO

DAY THREE

DAY FOUR

DAY FIVE

Figure 1.2   **Personal diary: What matters to me most in this school?**

Technical	Human	Educational	Symbolic	Cultural

Figure 1.3   Dimensions of school activity

What influences me most in my style of leadership?

This section aims to provide a way to examine the factors that are most significant as influencing factors on your role as headteacher.

We will do this by making a simple distinction between internally and externally motivated influence. Internal means the people, experiences, responsibilities and so on that you think were most important in your development. External means those influences that lie beyond school that have been most influential. These might be books, ideas, policies, a whole range of possible influences.

Figure 1.4 shows a matrix in which we encourage you to note down what aspects of internal and external influence have been salient factors in your development.

- What do you notice?
- Can you make any conclusions about the notes you have made?
- For example, do you find that previous headteachers appear as an internal factor that influenced you in your role as head?

Delve a little further into the responses that you have made. Do you find that you have been driven by positive role models and influences or negative

Inside school	Outside school

Figure 1.4   Influences on school
Source: Stoll and Clarke, 1995.

ones? Place a + or − against each response you identified. For example, was the influence or past experience of a headteacher positive or negative? Did they inspire you to lead like they did or never to do it again in that way?

The personal audit

We have been looking at the ways in which personal beliefs and attitudes influence and promote a particular style of working inside the school. This can show itself in the relationships between staff, between staff and pupils, the ways that management of decisions occur, the ways in which children relate to each other, the expectations we hold of ourselves and our colleagues, and in our linking of our internal school-based actions and those that have a direct bearing on the school in the wider community.

This section will continue with the theme of the headteacher and the personal audit by examining motivations and interpretations of the influences on the role.

The role of the headteacher

- What were the factors that made you want to be a headteacher?
- Have these been realised by subsequent actions that you have been able to take yourself?
- In what ways have these actions been manifest in visible things taking place in school?
- In what ways would you say that these things have remained hidden, or less visible, but are noticeable by you?
- In what ways do you feel that they have failed to materialise?
- What do I strive for within this role?
- How do current circumstances in school facilitate what I strive for?
- How do current circumstances inhibit what I strive for?
- Given your responses to these questions, what do you see as necessary action to ensure that your personal direction is to be met?
- What effect will this have on the school?

There are likely to be impacting factors on your actions for personal direction. Do they come into one of the areas of leadership that we refer to (see Figure 1.5)?

Looking at each of the areas, what actions might I personally need to take to effect this domain of leadership in a manner that fits with my personal goals?

What time-scale am I working on? In what ways will this positively effect the school?

Auditing the school culture

Hargreaves (1994) identifies different cultures of teaching. These cultures provide a context in which different strategies of teaching, and we might add broader strategies of managing change in school, are developed, sustained and preferred. The culture therefore grows to accommodate the various beliefs, values and habitual ways of doing things in school that become preferred forms of activity. Cultures in schools reflect many of the attributes of cultures in the wider sense of the term. They are historically embedded, they function collectively as shared actions, and serve to determine responses to external and internally originated change. To assume that they are a static phenomenon is to mistake their nature, just as to assume that there is a single school culture is to misunderstand the complex interaction that culture reflects.

We address culture here because it is within the context that we then might intend to introduce change. To do so assumes a degree of understanding of the context in which one is intending to act. The cultural context therefore plays an important role in determining the initial success of an agenda for change.

Technical	Human	Educational	Symbolic	Cultural

Figure 1.5   Areas of leadership

How might we use the understanding of culture to inform our view of school as we attempt to draw up a view of the dynamics of our school?

We suggest the following route as one possibility. It uses four reference points as extremes and indicates that there is a positional approach that the headteacher, or any member of staff, can take which will allow them to reflect on the contextual data they establish and then draw a conclusion as to the cultural profile based upon the information and their own perspective of the presenting problem.

Hargreaves (ibid.) recognises different types of culture in schools. These types of teacher culture are:

- fragmented individualism,
- Balkanisation,
- collaborative,
- contrived collegiality,
- the moving mosaic.

We now briefly provide a profile of each perspective.

Fragmented individualism: where we would see teachers working in isolation, having some protection from outside interference and influence, and where there would be an expected ceiling to improvement.

Balkanisation: where there are inconsistencies between different members of the staff in their approach and styles of working, where there are particular loyalties and identities that are tied to a particular group and the wholeness of the school matters less than the sum of its parts.

Collaborative cultures: operate with sharing, trust and a sense of support. This is underlying the daily work routine. There may be a strong family or paternalistic structure in place, there is emphasis on joint working and a continuous improvement ethos.

Contrived collegiality: where there would be a strategy that is recorded to improve collegiality, and similarly there would be a method of controlling that collegiality so that it remains within acceptable boundaries determined often by administrative procedures. There would be little in the way of risk taking and the organisation would not display strong desires to reshape.

Moving mosaic: where there would be blurred boundaries between different groups in the organisation. The members of one team might well be in a number of other teams and they would be dynamic and flexible in outlook, they would also display tendencies of uncertainty and vulnerability.

Taking an issue that you are particularly interested in pursuing within school, re-examine the dimensions that we have so far covered and relate them to the cultural perspectives that have just been described (see Figure 1.6).

What we want to do with these different dimensions is to explore further how we might now engage any one or a selection of them to move them in a direction that is desired.

Baselines

There is a considerable amount of interest in the baselining of school development. This is driven along by the perceived need to account for improvement by adding value to school actions. This is in our opinion singularly unhelpful if we are to look at schools as historically embedded organisations, with routines and cultures that perhaps extend back in time but which also project forward into as yet uncharted developments. The notion of a baseline can be a most misleading and uninvited simplification of a complex problem of making sense and meaning of a school and its personnel.

Baselines taken in this way are therefore only a simple pegging device that attempt to link certain key actions into a wider cultural context. The intention in this section is to ask some focal questions that relate closely to the positional idea of a baseline.

Style	Culture	Evidence to support this view
Technical leadership		
Human leadership		
Educational leadership		
Symbolic leadership		
Cultural leadership		

Figure 1.6   Cultural analysis table

What are the pressure points against which the school feels it needs to change? Are these pressure points self-generated or do they originate from beyond the school? If they are externally generated, what is the status of these external pressures? Are they mandatory? Are they optional? If these pressure points are optional, why do they feel so significant and on whose terms are they to be evaluated?

The crucial aspect of the baseline positioning of information concerns the degree of control that the school, and those involved in the school, and those with the responsibility to make future based judgements on the direction and pace of change, have over the pressure areas. There is a strong possibility that many of the changes that your school is involved in at the moment are ones that, given some serious reflection, might not be as important as first stated/declared, and an equally strong possibility that some fundamentally significant issues are not being addressed.

The leader in the school needs to ask a simple question of staff: is there a need for this change?

One indication of the need is to address the desires and wishes of staff. How do you know that staff want to institute a change in present working practices? Where do you get the evidence to justify these opinions?

The need for change – using the audit as an action-oriented device

The headteacher is well placed to act as a lead consultant because of the many people with whom they liaise during any given week in school.

Consider the following people when addressing the need for change, and the forms of evidence that you might draw upon in order to establish a base position with which you may want to plan and at a later stage revert back to.

- Staff
- Governors
- Pupils
- Parents
- Community
- LEA/External agencies

How might these different agencies best be consulted: by direct discussion, by letter, by telephone, by analysis of documentation, and so on?

Search for the forms of data that best suit the consulting group. It may be that they can come back to you with other and more suitable approaches if you approach them in a way that builds and engages them in the activity.

For what purpose is a change to be made?

A predictable outcome of an audit will be data that develop to inform you of the purpose of a change.

If the change has been internally proposed and developed, then you are by now beginning to gain an idea of the purposes behind the change. The critical issue here is whether it is a change – the replacement of one way of doing something with another – or an improvement – the introduction of a new way of doing something that has a stated purpose and an intention behind it.

It is here that we return to the end-in-mind that we described earlier. Revisit the concepts that were identified at that point. You have moved further in to an audit now and have gathered substantial amounts of information, both personal and school-wide. You should have gained a great deal more clarity over the focus, goals and approaches that might be most relevant to the innovation that is envisaged.

Are we clear about what we are changing?

- What is it that this change will do?
- What options exist for undertaking the change at this stage?

Are we clear about viewpoints and expectations related to the change?

- Who needs to know about the change?
- How will they be informed?
- Are the requirements and implications clear and do people involved understand them?
- How will opinions be gathered to establish if this is to be the case?
- What will be done with the outcomes that we gather?

We can consider these types of questions through three useful frames. The first concerns the structures that the change exists with and which the change might effect.

- Do people understand the implications of the changes to the school structure that the change will bring in?

The second concerns the roles that people will play after the change has been introduced.

- Do people have a clear understanding and appreciation of the kind of role that they will play once the change has been introduced?

The third concerns those key actions that need to take place in order that the change is effectively introduced. These key actions can relate to each other. An action that links coherently and consistently to a subsequent action, or a less simple change, an action that assumes a link into a more complex series of activities through which the person is expected to search for and establish next best routes. Key actions can also relate to structures. One key action might introduce a new set of reading books into the school library. The knock-on structural effects will be that these books are more popular, that they will be more likely to wear badly, so actions to reduce damage need to be placed into the school structure, together with some key actions regarding policy review on materials and perhaps loan times for books to ensure wide access to resources. There may be role changes that demand that the co-ordinator for reading in school has some time made available for author trails so that they can follow the extent to which certain authors are more popular. This in turn might mean that the curriculum planning team looks at the involvement of these books more into the central curriculum so they will need some planning time and so on ...

The point is that there is no such thing as a simple, one-off change when it comes to putting new initiatives in place. There will be plenty of visible implications and there will probably be equal amounts of unseen implications. To assist in this part of the audit Figure 1.7 has proved useful as it engages staff in deep-level discussions on the nature of the change, the structural effects and the role and key action effects. The activity need not take much time; it does however require careful unpacking in a group once the data is drawn together.

This technique allows staff to reperceive the problem that a particular change is raising. The use of the technique can assist the staff in identifying new possibilities within the change agenda, and it provides them with an important forum in which they are able to raise doubts about future plans.

It is most useful where there is a degree of uncertainty about the direction and implications of the change that is being proposed. By addressing the likely implications, both positive and negative, the people involved can begin to explore the clarity of the change as well as the implications about what it might most effect. Then, if the change is attempted, there is more likelihood that they will be seeking out the implications that they had predicted.

Linking the details of the change to the dynamics of organisational purpose and development

The second aspect of the technique that is valuable for strategic purposes is

Using positive and negative stimuli for forecasting change

What is the system? Do people know that they are part of the system? Who do we need to talk with? What key ideas have emerged?

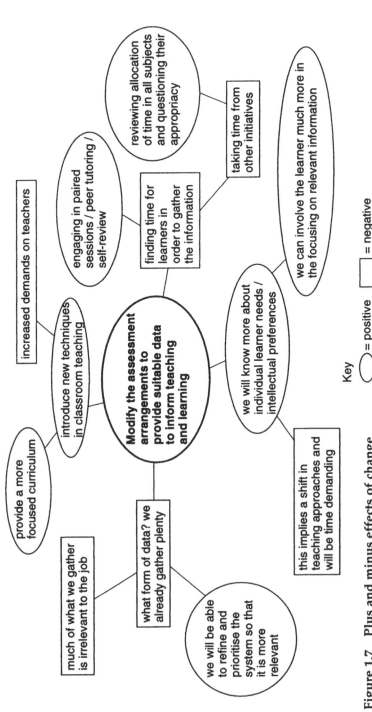

Figure 1.7 Plus and minus effects of change

that it can locate the change within a broader discussion of the organisational purpose behind the initiative. We explore a single theme, we develop it outwards from its initial implications and lead towards a wider and wider sphere of influences that are predicted, and staff can begin to correlate these implications with their collective and individual understanding of the organisational purpose. This action, of making connections between details and the dynamics of change, is a feature of the work of Senge (1990) when he describes the learning organisation.

Were we to model this aspect of the audit process we would be engaging in the following types of activity (bearing in mind the three focusing points of Structure, Roles, and Key actions).

1. Talk openly with colleagues about what you see as the purpose of the change.
2. Enquire what are the positive outcomes that we seek to establish as a result of our actions.
3. Enquire what the negative implications of the actions might be.
4. Investigate how this initiative will link with broader initiatives or parallel initiatives in school.
5. Where might there be clashes and problems with time, personnel, energy and so on?
6. How, given these considerations, will it contribute to the development of the school? What will it do and for whom will it do it?
7. Taking each of the components of leadership in turn, which of the six will be prioritised for particular attention during the innovation?
8. How are you planning to do this, and who will do this with you?

Looking at the school's past traditions related to the organisational change process

The idea of the school being rooted in experiences and actions based in the past has already been mentioned with reference to gathering baseline information. The intention in this aspect of the audit is to revisit the perceived and received view of school and to open discussions on this aspect of interpretation of the meaning of a change.

The most simple approach to address this area of school development is to ask: What are we known for here?

Ask this yourself based on your present knowledge of the school. It does not matter if you are new to the school or have been there for twenty years. You will be able to formulate a view.

Now ask yourself, based on what you know personally of the school, whether this is a fair interpretation of what the school represents. You might already be finding that it means different things to different people or groups.

If it is helpful, examine it against the cultural types, the leadership components or the linking of teacher, pupil, community, school, and personal.

D.H. Hargreaves (1995) offers a most useful modelling device (Figure 1.8) that can be used for plotting with staff their perception of the past, present and future orientation to a task in hand and expresses the social cohesion that is displayed through the maintenance of relationships. The power of the quadrant tool is that it can be applied personally, with a group or with the whole staff.

Each corner represents a different school type, four types being identified:

1. traditional: representing low social cohesion, high social control, custodial, formal, and unapproachable conditions;
2. welfarist: low social control, high social cohesion, relaxed, caring, cosy;
3. hothouse: high social control, high social cohesion, claustrophobic, pressurised, controlled;
4. anomic: low social control, low social cohesion, insecure, alienated, isolated and at risk.

These represent ideals rather than real culture because of the movement of schools. The model is useful because it enables staff to discuss, in practical and tangible ways, the influences of change on the deeper cultural dimensions of the school and, when applied to smaller facets of school life, similar discussion can occur at departmental level, or even provide analyses of subjects or year group approaches.

Figure 1.8   Quadrant tool
Source: D.H. Hargreaves (1995)

The preparation of a climate for change using staff development

This chapter has explored a series of simple but effective techniques that can stimulate discussion and focus attention upon different dimensions of school activity.

The implication that runs concurrent to the use of any of the techniques is that there is an overviewer, usually a member of a senior team in school, taking account of what is being discussed and using this to further develop the strategic planning, and to inform the nature and direction of the school change programme. The fundamental aspect of the approach to the techniques is that there is a deliberate use of the development of staff to foster a wider development at the school level.

This is a principal feature of the work that has gone on in recent years in the development of thinking on the learning organisation. In this conceptual model, the organisation and the individual are interdependent. There can be no organisational growth without individual growth and vice versa. Such an overarching philosophy demands that attention is paid to the needs of the person and of the school, that there is opportunity to renew and revisit aspects of the organisation and the personal work that is thought to be important, and that there is the potential within the organisation for risk-taking and creativity. The approach is a powerful metaphor for personal and organisational empowerment, where each member of the organisation is conscious of the collective and individual pressures to maintain and nurture achievement that all would value and wish to experience.

There are five components of the learning organisation as discussed by Senge (1990):

1. mental models,
2. vision/aspiration,
3. systems thinking,
4. team learning,
5. personal mastery.

The approach that we have taken so far in this book is to examine elements of each of these five parts of the learning organisation and to link them initially into the process of undertaking an audit of school.

This process of audit has been described as an examination of the positional stance from which subsequent actions might take place. We have pointed out that this is to investigate the personal view of the school and those factors that have influenced your role as a headteacher. These are all contextual data which frequently get missed in preference for the more transparent and tangible factors related to the day-to-day aspects of school performance. It is the task of the next chapter to move into the specific area of the role of the headteacher as a setter of targets, building upon those data which you have identified in relation to your own school as you have progressed through the material in this chapter.

Review question

Based on what you know about your school now, are there any significant issues that you need to revisit in this chapter before moving on?

2 Target setting: intention and purpose

Our theories determine what we measure ...
Albert Einstein

Introduction

When we set a target that we declare we intend to achieve, we make a public statement about our purpose and this in turn is informed by what we value. The act of allocating time to an initiative indicates that it matters sufficiently to want to do something about it. In the first chapter of this book we explored approaches that teased out those values and purposes that establish the influences, the motivation, the origin and directions of change. We were eager to point to those issues that prompted thinking on the personal as well as the organisational aspect of development, indicating that the mutual development of both the person and the organisation is desirable rather than development of one at the expense of the other. We were also interested in showing that there were two significant features of an audit:

- First, is to be able to make a clear view of where school is, where its strengths lie, where it shows signs of developing, and those areas of school that need further attention.
- Second, concerns the interpretative mindset which determines the types of questions that are being asked, and the subsequent conclusions as to the meaning of the data collected and the actions that then ensue.

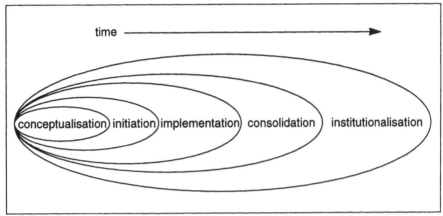

Figure 2.1   Different phases of change
Source: Fullan, 1991

The outcome of the audit will be a positional set of data upon which you can subsequently act. Having now spent time examining the purpose and reasoning behind what the school is doing through the process of an audit, an outcome of the audit may be that you now wish to promote a set of initiatives that are important in your view for the development of the school. If so, then the development is moving into a new phase of change from a conceptualisation phase into an initiation phase. It is useful to think about change in this way because different demands and needs will emerge as a result of the different considerations that will be involved. Whereas the conceptualisation phase was asking 'what' and 'why' questions, the initiation phase prompts practical questions associated with 'how' 'what if' 'could we try ...?'

We have illustrated this process in Figure 2.1 to locate this phase amongst the other identifiable phases of change. Question types at each stage of the process:

- Conceptualisation: What is happening here? Why does it happen like this?
- Initiation: What do we want to do as a result? How might we do it?
- Implementation: How are we doing it?
- Consolidation: What is helping this to work?
- Institutionalisation: Is there evidence that supports the success of this initiative?

Features of the initiation phase

During this phase targets will be clarified, selections will be made from the range of possible directions that the school can move in, strategies identified, time allocated, personnel identified, resources linked and appropriate action undertaken. This is probably an aspect of school life that you are most familiar with as it is a common process in schools, often directly linked to school development planning.

Establishing targets

Having briefly located the target-setting phase into a conceptual model of development of the school we will now reflect more closely upon the setting of targets and link this to the process of monitoring the effect of the work that is done.

Targets are important. Successfully planned targets make teams work together. They provide a common point of reference on which a team can focus together and try to achieve a set of common objectives. The sharing of a target is often a source of energy that activates a team and motivates and engages it to achieve outstanding performance.

In a study of the teacher's workplace Rosenholtz (1989) comments upon a number of reasons why targets were seen to have a significance in successful schools:

- Specific targets convey a message to teachers that they are capable of improvement.
- Specific targets provide a basis for rational decision making, for ways to organise and execute instruction.
- Specific targets enable teachers to gauge their success.
- Specific targets promote professional dialogue.

We will briefly elaborate on each of these themes because they serve well as a starting point through which to view the approach that effectively adopts and adapts targets to internal uses.

Specific targets convey a message to teachers that they are capable of improvement

The process of defining targets, establishing methods through which they will be achieved and then going about the business of achieving them is an empowering process where it carries with it the philosophy of involvement of staff. Target setting in collaboration with staff should be an enabling process that establishes a mindset of possibility and realisable achievement. It provides the headteacher with opportunities to create a culture in school that recognises that improvement can occur from within school, and that the staff themselves have the necessary control to determine and create the kind of school that they want to achieve.

There are downsides to target setting, which we will reflect upon later in this book, for the moment, we will consider the positive aspects of the approach.

Specific targets provide a basis for rational decision making, for ways to organise and execute instruction

Establishing a set of clear targets requires that we have a process of decision making. It is not a random effort. It is organised into a disciplined process that contributes to individual and collective understanding of the way that the school functions. The creating of targets therefore serves as an exemplary process for ways of doing things in school. Establishing specific targets demands organisational approaches and organisational and individual focus through the school, and it implies that there will be subsequent action taking place to achieve the targets. It therefore follows that staff will be thinking personally and collectively of their place within the decision making process and begin to target achieving process. This consciousness among staff of the targets and of day-to-day involvement in the process of an activity to achieve these targets is a lifeblood to a school as it improves. It avoids muddled messages because teachers can look at ongoing data gathered by monitoring the changes taking place in order to achieve the targets and they can share and respond together on what is happening.

Specific targets enable teachers to gauge their success

One of the difficult aspects of introducing change is to establish whether the change is having the desired effect, whether it is a success in the terms that staff defined as the targets were initially established. The area of reflective practice – of learning and reviewing past activity to inform future decisions – is one which is frequently left aside under pressure from other perhaps more immediately pressing issues. However, there is much to be gained from activity which tries to focus on the progress, small and large scale. By making the success a real part of the process of target setting, and making the small recognitions of success public, we are creating a culture that learns and looks for achievements. Again this is an incidental benefit of the process of target setting, but of profound importance to the development of the school climate that attaches significance to achievement.

Specific targets promote professional dialogue

Establishing a set of targets is a process not an event. If this process is to be valued and if the targets are to be of significance to the strategic development of the school, then there is a necessity that this process of target identification is facilitated through staff discussion. The nature of the targets, their potential to have a real impact on the school, and their likely effect on staff willingness to change are all important considerations of the discussions that might take place as the targets are established and subsequently worked on.

Target setting and wider development

As the previous section indicates, any target setting activity has to be a conscious effort to monitor the implicit and the explicit aspects of school development. There will be clear links between the targets that you set and the development of the school. Other subliminal aspects of the target setting exercise have the incidental effect of improving staff relationships, improving procedural activities in school, making communication routines more explicit, or just bringing people together more frequently to consider matters of whole school and team significance. These sub-texts of the core activity for planning school development are what we would describe as aspects of wider cultural development of the school. They are, however, vitally important to the success of the main targets and they therefore need to be nurtured and attended to as part of the monitoring activity that will take place as the targets are worked towards.

To support this wider developmental aspect of the target setting exercise reflect briefly on the following questions. If you find that you have not engaged in aspects of these issues with your staff team, ask yourself why, and what you might do to ensure that the implications of **not** doing so are not significant at a later stage.

- What is to be achieved?
- Has there been opportunity for all those involved to contribute to discussion on how this will be achieved?
- Has there been opportunity for those involved to explore their views on the benefits that are to come from the desired outcome?
- Have staff had a chance to consider the types of incidental information that might be useful?
- Is there a process in place to ensure that the staff can feed in their findings as the targets are worked towards?
- Have staff had the opportunity to discuss the local (direct effect of the change) and the global view (indirect wider agenda for change) of what is happening?

Targets, structures and cultures

Targets tend to be directed at improvements to school structures. That is, to make changes to the immediate, the visible and the tangible side of school activity. As well as these highly visible aspects of the process of target setting we would like to highlight the 'dark side' to change that is less tangible. This side concerns the school culture and it is observed in staff morale, relationships between people, the extent to which the staff feel motivated and eager to engage in activities that foster school or personal development.

The distinction between the two domains – the structural and the cultural – is important because they demand different forms of approach and awareness and because they pose quite different types of problems.

We can act to bring the awareness of the two domains into starker profile; indeed they interrelate all of the time. We cannot, for example, say that school culture does not matter and therefore does not exist on the change agenda, just as we cannot say that planning for the coming school year does not have to happen because we have 'done it before'. Both aspects need constant attention and nurturing. We use target setting activity to facilitate this process by:

1.   having clear targets in mind,
2.   establishing structures that are results oriented,
3.   establishing a culture that is results conscious,
4.   maintaining discussion on all aspects of the school development, from the mundane to the critical, in both formal and informal ways.

If our targets are clear, the structures which we have put into place are engaging staff and are focused towards target achievement. Our school culture will be reflected through staff awareness and consciousness of the opportunities available to optimise the achievements of the targets, and those targets will be met. Success or failure of target achievement is intimately linked with the activity of the school and staff. If attention is not paid to each element of the school then there will be limited long-term success. Success is reflected by a culture that is aware of the targets and is actively pursuing routes of reaching them effectively.

However, there are unpredictable aspects to target setting. It is worth reflecting briefly on the likely impact of this on the outcome of the target setting approach we choose to take. First of all, the target setting approach assumes that we can control change. This is a real chicken-and-egg phenomenon because, although our activity might cause change, the changes that we cause also cause us to change accordingly. The result is that target setting gives a seductive illusion of control which needs to be remembered when the school is dealing with complex change. Target setting can create organisational blinkers: it can inhibit the ability of the school to work as an organisation on the look-out for growth activity, because the focus can be so tightly defined by the development plan that anything that emerges as an alternative, or that challenges the present direction or pace of change in the school, might seem to be too much to have to deal with.

Success or failure in the achievement of targets is, in some ways, irrelevant. What matters far more is the ability of the school as a whole, and the individuals as part of the whole, to be able to identify factors and approaches that will assist in the general direction in which the school hopes to move.

Where is the target located?

The first task concerned with target setting is to determine what aspect of school life the activity will be addressing. Having a sense of what we are 'aiming for' may sound obvious, but it is quite possible that a vague notion of 'doing something about reading performance in Key Stage 1' is sufficient to cause significant effort and later considerable frustration when we begin to ask: 'Well, what exactly is it going to do?'

Active inquiry

The technique that we can use to initiate a sense of clarity about the target is to inquire of the intention. This involves applying a series of simple questions to the specific focus of the intention. It serves to locate the thinking on the target and the implications of the target.

Question: What exactly are we trying to do?

Approach: Listen to the responses from colleagues. Try to establish the common threads between responses. One method that can facilitate the success of the listening is to map the conversation through key points that your colleague makes from the conversation. Start in the centre of a page and work outwards, linking together any ideas that emerge. When a new idea is proposed, begin a new strand of links. At the end of the discussion spend a few minutes with your colleague reflecting on the conversation and the key points. Highlight the ones that you both accept as being the most helpful in defining the purpose of the target.

An example from a discussion with a Year 2 teacher:

Q: What exactly is the target that you are aiming for?
R: We are hoping to improve the reading results at the end of Key Stage 1.

Q: I see so you want to improve the reading results. Do you mean that you want to improve the results of all pupils?

R: No, we want to get all children to a base position of level 2 or above.

Q: I see, so it is specifically those children that are at the lower end of the performance that you are focusing on. What will you do in order to identify those children?

R: Well, we plan to use the teacher assessment data, and observational information that we have gathered through class activities, and information from our reading programme.

Q: So there will be two main types of data – teacher assessment data and classroom activity data ... I see ... now can we move to the issue of improvement of performance ... What do you intend to do to improve the performance of these pupils?

R: Well, we plan to have a paired reading activity where older children from the junior classes will be assigned a younger child to read with them and share stories for a set time each day, an increased teacher involvement with them along the lines of a reading recovery scheme, and to provide them with more out of school support through an education extra out of school club where they can get help and support from parents and assistant staff.

Q: So what specifically might you look for in these activities that will inform you of the success of the approach? [... *continues* ...]

The first part of the discussion with the Year 2 teacher addressed the target area that she was intending to tackle. You will note that initially this was extremely wide. She had an idea but she had not focused in on the details of the target from the outset.

The approach to the questioning is important. There is no judgement made of the things which the teacher promotes, merely a search for confirmation of intent and clarity. You are seeking clarification and detail, not making or stating preferences for why this is the target.

Question: *Can you tell me a little more about ...*

There is a fair amount of repetition of the teacher's own terminology. This serves to indicate to her that you are focused in on her issue. It enables the discussion to flow more purposefully. Each time, the question closes in on specifics: for example, all children or some, or what specifically will you look for?

Question: *What specifically do you mean by ...?*

The selection of the question is not accidental. It is deliberate and attempts to tease out the specific points that form the target that is being discussed.

What will the target most likely effect?

Exploration into the focus of the target will initiate a second line of inquiry that can be extremely useful for staff to locate the target and begin to examine possible sources of information that can reveal if it is being achieved. Doing this will alert colleagues to the many different forms of information that we can draw upon for our appreciation of the effect of a target.

Question: What will most likely be effected by achieving the target?

Staff might look for changes in:

- the ways that people communicate with each other,
- the physical feel of the working environment,
- the clarity of documentation that they receive,
- the way they see their role,
- the amount of time that is needed to undertake the task now from before,
- better uses of limited resources,
- pupils' approach to their work,
- pupils being actively engaged in learning tasks,
- pupil behaviour,
- a mood of optimism and enthusiasm that is different.

As is evident, the range of outcomes will be vast. The greater the range of initiatives, the more difficult it will be to determine the likely effects, but the exercise is useful because staff are beginning to think about change with the end in mind, rather than thinking about change as a permanently open-ended exercise.

Target setting and people

In this activity we are seeking to develop the awareness of staff to the many effects of change. We are asking the question:

- Who will this change effect?

This raises a number of considerations about the organisational effect of the target and the likely implications for staffing and responsibility changes that might result.

As a starting point, you might find that a simple list of people that are involved in the change can begin this discussion. Secondly, and following on immediately from the 'who' question, is:

● What will the change most likely effect?

Again, a brainstorming activity frequently opens up the links between the impact and effect of the change. Address structures and culture in the detail of response. Keep in mind the purpose behind the activity:

1. To raise collective awareness of the target that has been set, the persons who will be effected, the impact on other aspects of school;
2. To initiate the discussions that can lead to data gathering to inform the success of the target.

An alternative way of approaching this issue is to consider the specific location through predefined headings:

● Where is your target most suitably located?

Write a brief description of your target in the cell in Figure 2.2 that best fits.

Does the target also link into the other targets in any way? For example, does a primary Curriculum target have a secondary link to a Human target because it involves some specific training?

Seek out ways that the five areas can assist your definition and locating of the problem.

Whose targets are these?

Often the origin of the target has a bearing on the final impact. The most likely external target for the individual school is going to come from the Ofsted inspection and subsequent key areas for action.

If a school staff are confident and determined as a team, they might find that internal targets are far better realised than those that are initiated by an external body. For example, the Ofsted key areas for action might identify a number of issues that the school had already considered as being relevant for development. The external targets then merely reinforce the internal intentions. However, if the external targets differ from those which the school feels it should be focusing upon, there is more likely to be difficulties in persuading colleagues.

The school improvement targets which will emerge as a result of the recent white paper (HMSO, 1997) are more than likely to be set as external targets. These are to be school defined and externally ratified. The important point to consider here is how realistic, how achievable, and how challenging

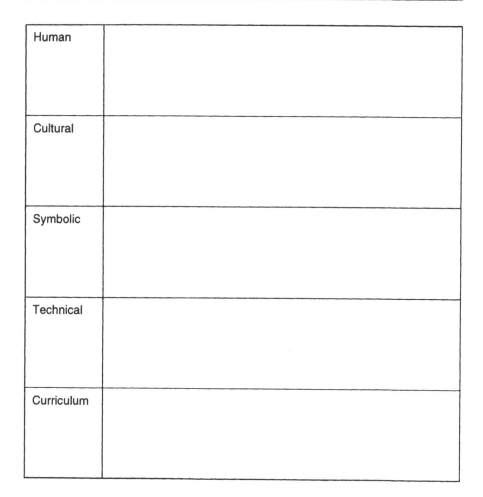

Human	
Cultural	
Symbolic	
Technical	
Curriculum	

Figure 2.2   Location of the target – where do you hope the effect will be felt?

these targets actually become, particularly in relation to the direction that the school wishes to move in and the extent to which these targets reflect real internal motive, rather than a contrived version of the external targets.

Identifying the source of a target

There is always going to be something that originates from outside the school to inspire or put pressure on other developmental activity in the school. It is useful to develop an awareness of these external targets because, utilised carefully, they can be operationalised internally to further other school-based development. The process of investigating the external and internal sources of the target is outlined in Figure 2.3. The internal modification required to achieve the target is then considered.

Knowing something about the target in this way allows a discussion to then examine the possible internal applications and modifications that are necessary to further other initiatives that the school might already have in hand. Hopkins et al. (1994) describe this linkage between external and internal activity as an act of consonance.

The target is described.
The intention of the target is identified – what is it meant to do?
The impact of the target is examined
Who will it affect?   What will it affect?

Figure 2.3   External to internal sources of the target

Some questions to consider

- How does this target originating from an external source support any of our internal change efforts?
- Where does this fit in with other targets?
- What results will you look for that can act as evidence of achievement?
- What results will you look for in school which will indicate that the target has achieved a cultural change?
- To whom might we need to report progress and how frequently?

Modelling the thinking: designing the process

We have started this chapter by addressing the location of targets. We now move to addressing the shaping of thinking that guides approaches to target setting and targeting action to meet them. This sharing of thinking with staff will initiate activity to ensure that they are contributing to the strategic approaches and the supportive thinking that the school is making in response to targets.

Times of change are stressful times. People get anxious and uncertain of how change will affect them. They are unsure of the details of their own role, they might have reservations and nagging doubts about the relevance of the targets. Often the present state of the school looks better than the one that it is proposed the school will move into or towards. This means that there will need to be care and concern expressed for the people involved in the 'doing' of the change. A change plan may determine that the change will be in place in six weeks' time at the end of the first half-term of the new school year, but if staff are not feeling good about the change, and have not had sufficient opportunity to explore their concerns and doubts personally and collectively, there is no doubt that these concerns will magnify and will return at a later stage and impede the efforts taken.

The following activity provides an opportunity for colleagues to reflect on these concerns constructively by placing them within a context of time.

Just think for a moment about times in your own career when you have met resistance to changes that you wanted to introduce.

- What was voiced by colleagues at that time?
- What were the main themes of their resistance?
- Why do you think that this was so?
- What did you do in response?

Place the present concerns into an historical timeline.
Some further questions:

- When were the present changes first discussed?
- When were the concerns about the change (however small) discussed?
- What was suggested or done in response to these concerns?
- Did this have the desired effect?
- Why? Why not?
- What would you suggest happens now?
- What would you like to see happen in the future?

These questions describe personal feelings about matters that affect the school or the individual teacher. The benefits of such conversations are that they make some of the unspoken aspects of school life clearer. They enable staff to see that there are processes in place, or able to be put in place, which can facilitate their voice in both formal and informal settings to influence the nature of the change in the school.

Sharing strategic approaches

One supportive technique that can easily be introduced into the work with colleagues is to share strategic approaches to the problems being faced. This enables each team member to have a better insight into the steps that are expected to be taken. It offers the opportunity for members of the team to feed in further thoughts on contributions that they might make to the process of achieving the goal and developing the learning of the staff as a team.

This section will illustrate an approach that can be taken to the introduction of the change and it will indicate where there are possible areas for growth as that process develops.

A developmental approach to sharing thinking

After you have established targets, you will need to ensure that you meet these targets effectively. This takes the change discussions from the initiation stage into the implementation stage. To determine whether you have appropriately structured the process of change, it is necessary to create a cross-referenced map of the relationships between the people, tasks and timing to illuminate to all involved the step-by-step process that will move the organisation towards the target (see Figure 2.4).

The purpose behind this first activity is to avoid the often heard claim that 'there is no agreed process ... it just seems to get done'.

Process design stages

The following section will present an analytical framework to assist you in

SCHOOL DEVELOPMENT PLAN

SECTION 2.4.1   INTRODUCTORY STATEMENT

Organisation

Number per Year Group

Mrs. Gray	22 pupils	(R15 & Y1 7)	Reception	15
			Year 1	24
Mrs. Cartwright	26 pupils	(Y1 17 & Y2 9)	Year 2	9
			Year 3	22
Miss Ayre	42 pupils	(Y3 22 & Y4 20)	Year 4	20
			Year 5	25
Miss Hartley	40 pupils	(Y5 25 & Y6 15)	Year 6	15
	—			—
	130			130

Following staff discussions and backing from the Governors to maintain the separation of K.S.1 and K.S.2 children we will have two very large classes. Y4/Y5 – 42 pupils, and Y5/Y6 – 40 pupils. These classes will require constant monitoring and the staff given support to alleviate the difficulties of working with such large numbers.

Numbers in the K.S.1 classes will be lower; Reception/Y1 – 22; Y1/Y2 – 26. The alternative of dividing the n.o.r. by four (teachers) would have given average sizes of 32 per class but one class would have consisted of 3 age groups and children from K.S.1 and 2 which was clearly very undesirable from the teaching point of view and from a parent's point of view. The Governors felt very strongly that such class groupings would lead to some parents taking their children elsewhere where the classes might be large but at least the children were all the same year group.

Support for the *K.S.2* classes will be given by:
   employing an N.T.A. to assist work in the classes;
   involvement of voluntary/parental help in class;
   time-table commitment from the Headteacher;
   time-tabled non-teaching time for the teachers;
   commitment of financial resources wherever required;
   close liaison between Head/Deputy Head and teachers;
   providing Inset for K.S.2 teachers if requested.

Figure 2.4   **Represents a process map that shows a typical linear development process**

SCHOOL DEVELOPMENT PLAN

SECTION 2.4.2   PRIORITIES

Completed Priorities '94–'95

The S.D.P. priorities for '95–'96 follow from whole-staff discussion, the unfulfilled priorities from the '94–'95 S.D.P. and N.C. requirements.

The achievements reached in the '94–'95 plan were:
　English Policy Document – completed;
　Appraisal Policy – completed;
　Music Policy Document – completed;
　Information Technology Policy Document – completed;
　New N.C. documents – read and discussed by staff;
　S.E.N. Policy Document – completed;
　Differentiation Policy Document – completed;
　Prospectus Review commenced.

Other achievements were:
　Teacher Assessment Portfolio – Maths;
　Library Organisation;
　Introduction to Ofsted procedure;
　First Appraisal cycle;
　Setting up of playgroup in school;
　Re-organising to four classes.

Priorities for '95–'96

Items unfinished in '94–'95 which will become priorities for '95–'96 include:
　Behavioural Policy Document,
　R.E. Policy Document;
　Health Education Policy – Review;
　Prospectus Review.

Other areas identified by staff as priorities for '95–'96 are:
　Record of Achievement – Review;
　English Policy Review;
　Maths – Review;
　I.T. Review.
　Science – Review;
　P.E. Policy Document;
　Technology Review;
　Geography Policy Document;

Figure 2.4 *continued*

SCHOOL DEVELOPMENT PLAN

SECTION 2.4.3   CURRICULUM AND OTHER PRIORITIES (CONTINUED)

SPRING TERM

PRIORITY (What?)	ACTION		SUCCESS CRITERIA (How? What?)	FINANCE / RESOURCES (How much?)	STAFF DEVELOPMENT (What?)
	(Who?	When?)			
R.E. Policy Document	W. Smith	Spring Term	Whole school staff meetings – written document	Paper, Source books for teachers. Possible purchase of artefacts.	Advisory Teacher involvement has already been used.
Health Education Policy Document	W. Smith	"	Whole school staff meetings – written document	Paper. Source material.	
Technology – Review	A. Hartley	"	Whole school staff meetings. – is N.C. being covered? – adopt changes – consider further Inset	Possibly source material for teachers. Possibly more equipment and materials.	
Science – Review	J. Cart- wright	"	Is current practice fulfilling N.C. requirements? Adopt any changes	Possibly source material for teachers.	

Figure 2.4 *continued*

SCHOOL DEVELOPMENT PLAN

SECTION 2.4.3   CURRICULUM AND OTHER PRIORITIES (CONTINUED)   SUMMER TERM

PRIORITY (What?)	ACTION (Who?)	ACTION (When?)	SUCCESS CRITERIA (How? What?)	FINANCE / RESOURCES (How much?)	STAFF DEVELOPMENT (What?)
P.E. Policy Document	J. Ayre	Summer Term	Whole school staff meetings on the policy	Paper	Implementation of knowledge and skills gained from D.F.E. 10 day P.E. Course – J. Ayre
Geography Policy Document	W. Gray	"	Whole school staff meetings on the policy	Paper. Teaching source material possibly	

Figure 2.4 *continued*

SCHOOL DEVELOPMENT PLAN

SECTION 2.4.3   CURRICULUM AND OTHER PRIORITIES

AUTUMN TERM

PRIORITY (What?)	ACTION		SUCCESS CRITERIA (How? What?)	FINANCE / RESOURCES (How much?)	STAFF DEVELOPMENT (What?)
	(Who?)	When?			
Record of Achievement – Review	W. Smith/ W. Gray	Autumn Term	Whole school staff meetings – adopt changes	Possible reprint. Enough paper in stock.	Review rewards system as whole staff
Behaviour Policy Document	W. Smith	"	Whole school staff meetings – written document	N/A	
Topic Planning – Review	W. Gray	"	Whole school staff meetings. – is it detailed enough? – adopt changes	N/A	
English Document – Review	W. Smith	"	Whole school staff meetings – adopt changes	N/A	
Maths – Review Documentation	J. Cart- wright	"	Whole school staff meetings. – update present document	Possible reprint. Enough paper in stock.	

Figure 2.4 *continued*

SCHOOL DEVELOPMENT PLAN

SECTION 2.4.4   STAFF DEVELOPMENT

Staff Development

Staff Development is carried out through weekly Curriculum Development meetings; Inset Courses; the use of non-pupil Days and when appropriate the use of Advisory Teachers.

During the current financial year the school is a subscriber to the L.E.A.'s Inset Programme.

Staff Development is organised to address the needs of individual teachers, which might be identified through Appraisal, and the needs of the school. Priority will also be given to the needs of members of staff who will be changing year groups in September.

Non-pupil Days '95–'96

4.7.95	a.m.	Professional Duties
	p.m.	Staff Planning Meeting – The School Calendar 95/96
8.1.96	a.m.)	I.T. Review – whole school review of new equipment
	p.m.)	and operation of programmes etc.
2.5.96	a.m.	P.E. Policy
	p.m.	Curriculum Development follow-up.
3.5.96	a.m.) p.m.)	Don Valley Pyramid Day

"Extra" Curriculum Meetings

3 x 2 hours after school meetings in lieu of non-pupil Day on the last day of Summer Term 1996 (Monday 22nd July!)

1. Autumn Term   Whole-staff visit to Austerfield Study Centre
2. "   "   Maths Review – bring up to date present policy document in line with new N.C.
3. Spring Term   Science Review – ditto

Figure 2.4 *concluded*

locating a change within a longer term linear process. The purpose is to offer a model against which your developmental activity might be reviewed and reconsidered.

Each stage is described, then there are a series of pointers which show the types of activity and thinking that are likely to be taking place in each of the stages of the process.

1. Defining the setting

QUESTION: What is happening here? What matters about this?
ACTIONS: Looking, listening
APPROACH: Open and reflective
SEEKING: Viewpoints and concepts, contrasting and conflicting viewpoints

This phase requires that the staff are involved in identifying from current work arrangements those aspects of the work that might need modification or development. This approach is necessarily open-ended, exploratory and can be a continual part of school culture.

Once an issue is identified, then it can be focused upon and the question can be asked whether change is needed and if so, what needs to be done.

2. Redefining the situation

QUESTION: What do we now understand of the problem?
ACTIONS: Desynthesising viewpoints, representing the newly understood 'whole', rationalising, strategising, designing and looking at parts of the whole.
APPROACH: Focused and intent on clarification, and confirmation of view.

Following the problem-seeking time described in phase one, we enter into a time where it is necessary to draw together the findings and make sense of the change that is desired. This is an important part of defining the target – stating what it will be like, and building a rationale for why it is necessary within a larger whole of the school development.

3. Stirring up the situation

QUESTION: Concerned with the process – how is this going?
ACTIONS: Practical involvement, intent on making the change real so looking for evidence of success
APPROACH: Transitional, comparing old with new

At the third phase of the process we are starting to undertake change. We expect unexpected outcomes and we are looking out for examples that we can use to inform our understanding of what is happening. We are seeking information on the immediate feelings and responses of staff to the change in comparison between the new changes and the old ways of doing things.

4.   Hearing the responses

QUESTION: What do you feel about this?
ACTIONS: Formal and informal opinion seeking
APPROACH: Listening, non-judgemental, conscious of the cultural effect of the change as well as the structural effect

5.   Reconstructing

QUESTION: What do we think of it so far?
                     Formal feedback
                     Informal feedback
ACTIONS: Learning at the individual and the organisational level about the process and its positive and negative impact
APPROACH: Hypothesising and evaluative

6.   Redefining the setting

Re-presentation of the situation

QUESTION: Now that we know what we can do, how will we take our work forward?

The process is deliberately outlined in such a way as to prompt thinking on the thinking, plans and subsequent activity that happen as a consequence of any developmental activity.

Targeting implementation

This part of the target setting process is often undertaken through discussion and recording of key outcomes. The linking of the two together will provide a useful shared mental model of the intention and approaches that are decided.

Establishing a base position

Step one: Describe the process of change as you think it will proceed. This is going to be a base position representing where the school is today. You may have data that you can draw upon from the audit that informs this position. You may wish to start from this point and move into an audit or move directly into an action in school. Either way this is a representation of the here and now.

Step two: Describe the target and locate it on the map. This is going to be the target point that you hope to reach through actions that will take place in between the base position and the target position. It is useful to be specific here about this end-target. Is it a technical, human, educational, symbolic or cultural target? Is it a mix of these? If so, specify how you think it is reflected in the labels. This helps to locate the target in activity and experience that is also in the present. Targets that seem to be plucked out of the air have less chance of success. They are far riskier because they have no commonality of experience through which they can flourish. The more that the target can be contextualised the better.

Step three: Identify and locate the key sub-targets. See Figure 2.5. This highlights the reason for separate sheets of paper as each sheet might contain details at a later stage and being separate it can be moved about.

Now start to fill in as best you can the sub-targets that will be taking place as the change is introduced. At this point be more concerned to get a sequence that you feel is relevant and realistic than detailing exactly when and who is involved.

Step four: Identify the function targets. These are the smaller targets that support the achievement of the sub-targets. They can be identified by asking the question: what do we do that contributes to achieving the sub-target?

Step five: Make the information public. Leave the recorded details in a prominent place on the wall in the staffroom for a period of time to facilitate discussion and awareness. If you assume that this period of defining and setting targets will take twice as long as you predicted, you will be starting to pace the introduction realistically. Ensuring that staff have sufficient time and space to engage formally (through meetings and planned activity linked to the change) and informally (through 'corridor' discussion) is vital. If you don't build this space into the process then there will undoubtedly be a point when staff will take their own time out anyway. Be aware of the need for this and make it a frequent part of the change agenda.

Leaving the information on the staffroom wall, or in the planning room, or wherever it is publicly accessible enables staff to look at it, add notes and ideas that might have been overlooked. It also provides an opportunity for

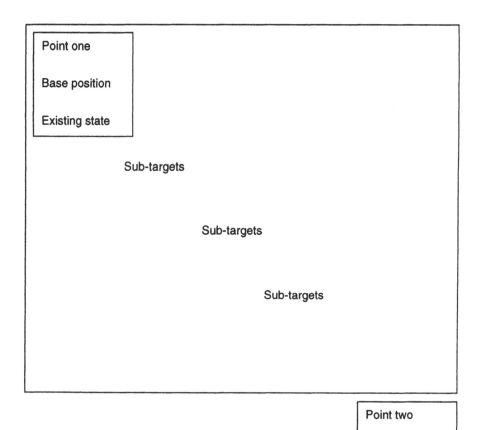

Figure 2.5   A linear progress map

staff to reflect and enables them to begin to assimilate the overall plan of action.

Step six: Time and personnel.   This refers to the detailed information necessary to put the process into action. It demands a focused session, prepared with staff being fully informed of the purpose of the meeting and with an agenda circulated beforehand to ensure attendance and pre-session thinking.

Step seven: Separate process management from performance management.   Having established a route forward, it may now assist the day-to-day development of the work by identifying the specific milestones of the process. These can serve as formal reporting times for the development.

The details of the performance management (i.e., what people will need to do in order to reach the targets) can be separately investigated and discussion can take place on the ways in which the performance can be improved based upon the flow chart of the process.

Outcomes

The outcome of this process management activity is a facilitative set of material which visually represents a real process that the staff are going to work their way through over a given period of time.

The purpose behind the activity is to establish management of a process of change through the setting of targets. In effect we are setting up procedural approaches that allow the change to be managed on an ongoing basis rather than a 'fix when broken' approach. This approach demands that we have an infrastructure upon which staff can reflect and realign their micro-practice to ensure that the targets are achieved and equally important that members of the team are involved throughout in the design, development, planning, implementation and actions in getting to the targets.

The key process management questions that you need to ask of yourself and your staff are:

- Do you understand your process?
- Have you established appropriate process sub-targets?
- How will you manage the process?
- Have sufficient resources been allocated to the process and each set of sub-targets?
- When one sub-target leads into another, are you satisfied that the link points will be managed?

Review of the procedures

Make sure that people understand the process by graphically representing the activities (mapping).

Try to contain the sub-targets and the functional targets so that they are recognisable elements on the route of the development, and not blurred over long time periods. If some elements do blur over time, be aware of them. Mark them up as fuzzy areas that need particular attention. Try to explore ways that you might monitor the impact of these sub-targets.

Recording change journeys: monitoring change effects over time

Having established the location of a target, and the approaches that you feel are relevant to take, the process of 'stirring up the setting' becomes the next phase of the activity. In this phase of implementation, we engage in activity to achieve sub-targets. This is a critical part of the process, and one that is often left to happen, because people know what they are to do and how they should proceed and there is a tendency to take the pressure off the initiative and let it loose. This is a critical time because it is a movement from the security of a planned schema, to a real time, real life scenario. Techniques must be developed that will capture the essence of the implementation to identify those aspects that function well and those that need revisiting.

There are many ways to record the process of change. Those which seem to have most success are those which translate into day-to-day school life in such a way that they become routinised, and at the same time capture useful information in sufficient quality and detail to inform staff discussion.

One important aspect of change-related information is to ensure that the interpretation we subsequently make of the information we gather on that change is sufficiently coherent that people can make sense of it, without it being so detailed as to be unmanageable. This is a difficult balancing act. Information that is gathered needs to inform and therefore demands explanation. From our own work we suggest that the explanations will change over time as deeper understanding and knowledge of the change and its connections to other changes and activity within school take place. This implies that an important characteristic of any techniques that are used to support the interpretation of change will be brevity, followed by relevance to the task in hand. That task, for our purposes, is to inform discussion on the progress of change. Schools that do not involve themselves in feedback activity such as monitoring the impact of change remain oblivious to data that could be coming to them and are therefore insensitive and non-responsive to feedback. This lack of inclination to self-modification leads to situations where they become increasingly externally change-driven because external forces are the only point of reference they have for any monitoring.

It is quite possible to learn to use monitoring techniques, from the simple to complex. They only require a little time and can soon become invaluable tools in a school's repertoire for improvement.

A useful technique we have found records a sense of change of school activity over time. This technique is the timeline (see Figure 2.6).

This technique is simple to adopt and is useful because it imposes a strict linear sequence on significant issues. The timeline identifies change events through a 'label'. For example it might record in the event row that an agreement trial took place. Involvement could be across the whole staff.

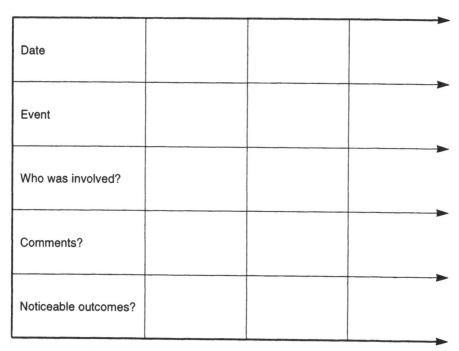

Figure 2.6   Timeline structure

Comments could address the focus of the activity and the outcomes column could note down the action points to be addressed and decisions that were made for the next meeting.

This form of timeline does have limitations. First, it makes change appear linear when it often is not. This is difficult because sometimes events last over longer periods of time, with a drip-in effect rather than a single meeting.

To overcome the linear feel of the timeline there are options for modifying the timeline by adding links and loop back to earlier, similar events. Or modelling the timeline in a slightly different way as demonstrated in Figure 2.7.

Running the timeline and identifying multiple events enable each event to be plotted in time. Then the overlapping events are more noticeable as they locate along the line. This can provide valuable visual evidence of overload periods, as well as indicating periods in which there appears less in the volume of change but perhaps a good deal of practical groundwork taking place.

A timeline is only as useful and developmentally beneficial as the effort involved and the applications for which it is used. But evidence from recent work using the timeline over sustained periods (Clarke and Christie, 1996)

	Date	Date	Date	Date	Date
Event 1					
Event 2					
Event 3					
Event 4					
Comments					

Figure 2.7　Timeline structure no. 2

indicates that it can be a significant tool when staff are trying to link improvement intentions to wider activity. The value lies in the timeline being an open-ended device: you can enter as little or as much detail as required and it doesn't always have to be on the same event.

For example, one school used the timeline to locate all of the activities linked to the school development plan. Each activity was colour coded, and the teachers were able to see quite quickly the link between targets that were achieved because there was sufficient development time, and others that faltered because they clashed with peak times across school or were just badly timed or not relevant at that point. The school has subsequently developed the timeline to include real versus expected time. So the timeline has a planned line already visible for the events that will take place over the year, and then a real timeline of the events as they actually happen. The leverage into dialogue over the inconsistencies between the two points, planned and real, is useful because it raises the awareness of the conflicts and dilemmas that are faced as a school moves on an improvement journey.

Ripple effects and monitoring change

A variation on the timeline technique is one that approaches planned changes as a series of overlapping or conflicting ripples.

This technique locates the target as the centre of a ripple. Each 'ring' that moves out from the target is a successive event of significance. Working backwards from the target enables staff to model a single line of events, and to then successfully cross-reference those with other events taking place in the same time frame. This time frame can be a term, a half-term, a two-week period, a week or even in some cases a daily introduction.

The advantage of this type of model is that it is open to considerable 'influence' mapping as the target is neared.

Using the template in Figure 2.8 locate a key target in the central circle. In subsequent circles locate influential actions that you will be involved in to achieve the target. Continue with one or two influences at most on each of the ripples. Add as many as you require until you feel that you have modelled the outward effects. Now locate those outer effects to a timescale. Add what you think are other relevant notes and comments.

A development of this technique, and a more sophisticated application, is to look at the impact of other ripple effects in school. This adopts the idea that with more than one initiative taking place in school at any given time there will be positive and negative knock-on effects. The interlocking of different ripple maps can facilitate thinking in this area of target setting.

Ask staff to reflect on the first ripple map that you have created. Now ask

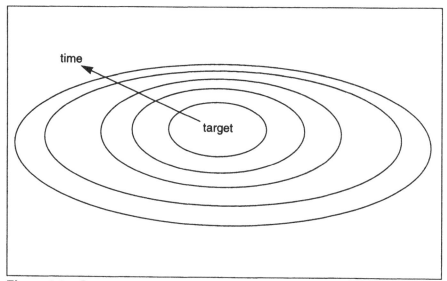

Figure 2.8   Open target mapping

Is this a problem linked to:				
technical issues	human issues	educational issues	symbolic issues	cultural issues

Figure 2.9   Locate the problem

them to develop a second overlapping map that links to another initiative. Where do the problems become apparent? Use the chart in Figure 2.9 to guide your analysis of the problems.

- Are they to do with timing?
- Are they to do with energy? (e.g. people will not do as much at the end of a long term as they would at the start)
- Are they to do with personnel?
- Are they to do with other resources?
- Are they to do with the nature of the events?
- Are they to do with personality and team groups?

Other techniques that can assist the target setting and monitoring of the change process

Mindmapping techniques

This technique simply requires those involved in the change to meet together frequently and locate the target into the weave of different initiatives and influences that are prevalent at that time. A record is kept and staff can refer back to it at a later stage for review and development activity.

Flow diagrams

This technique is based on the use of flow charting. Sequences, order, phases, directions and repeating events are located and the maps are added to at each revisit of the target activity.

Theme maps

The key milestone points are located on a timeline and then linked themes are spidered off the sub-target points. The advantage of this approach is that forward planning to the next target can be realigned to the target if there are signs that the target is being missed in any way.

Classification maps

Classification maps describe the attributes of the target. They will refer to the following:

- target: purpose,
- sub-targets: strategies to achieve,
- actions: timing/resources/personnel/outcome required.

These provide a useful précis of the target and make good briefing material for all staff even if only some of the team are directly involved.

Cluster maps

This is another technique that allows ongoing processes to be located and links to be identified in advance and as the project proceeds. The use of different colours is valuable in this type of map both because additional modifications can be most useful for future reference and as additions to new target setting activity. They are good for creating staff awareness of the non-linear nature of planning to achieve targets because they raise the fact that there is a degree of incremental modifying and innovation that takes place on the change journey.

Each of these techniques enable staff to focus upon the changes that are to be taking place as a target is worked towards. They enable the attention to be sustained against each sub-target whilst the end is kept in mind.

Pushing the frontier – the longer term implications for the head and the organisation

There are many ways that change can be introduced but many of these are flawed by lack of sensitivity to the people who work in the school, and a lack of purpose and intention. In order to move a school forward with any real meaning it is important to realise that there will be fluctuations in pace, quality and performance of staff. This does not reduce expectations, but it makes the possible realisable and the impossible more accepted because human needs are being catered for as well as simply the organisational.

An holistic view of school improvement recognises that human beings operate within active, dynamic and ultimately self-organising systems in a much more positive way than if their actions are totally controlled and determined. The implication for target setting is clear: not to over-determine; to allow scope for continuous growth; and to realise and expect the unexpected as well as the planned. The ability to deal with continual change will be better incorporated in school where there is a degree of both self-reflection and organisational reflection. This in turn implies that efforts will be made to engage in discussions that are more than just the 'plan and deliver' approach to change that has been such a feature of recent developmental working response to policy demands.

If the efforts of the school can consider the possible school, and not just the planned and likely school, then opportunities exist for school staff to develop new skills that seek out:

- interconnectedness – where there are many relationships between developments and events and there is more than just an intellectual understanding of such links. It is something that a successful team will describe as a feel for the right direction to take.
- a sense of identity in the group and a sense of personal role – where there is a sense of purpose and coherence of value and belief which is expressed at the personal and the group level.
- a scope for the growth of each other as well as the organisation – where staff are reaching out to learn more of what is happening and this in turn allows them to learn more purposefully and beneficially for the school as well as for themselves as they are gaining insights and new ways of approaching old problems.
- an ability to better deal with uncertainty – where the staff have the freedom to express their viewpoints on change, and they are engaged in the process of setting and monitoring targets with a view to continual improvement, they will be more able to respond to subtle changes in

demand and will recognise and talk through some of the problems that paradoxical change can bring.

Applying the learning so far ... a simulation activity

Planning at Trenchtown

Trenchtown Junior and Infant School has decided that it is going to introduce a portfolio assessment system in the coming school year. The system is intended to run as a pilot for the first year across three of the five teaching groups. This enables all ages of pupils to be targeted, but does not have to involve all staff all of the time in the development. Indeed, one member of staff is already involved in the activity which means that she will need to be informed of progress but not directly involved. There is an intention to review after the first six months, and then a major review at the end of the year with a view to full implementation the following year. It is now mid-spring term and plans are that the process should begin to be put into place so that work can take place during the summer for autumn implementation.

Staff include five teachers, the headteacher teaches 0.5 of the time and there is one non-teaching classroom assistant. Between the present time and the autumn term there are two days available for staff training, and one of these has been allocated to the development of the portfolio. There are other opportunities to meet and plan in the forthcoming six staff meetings which will be one hour in length.

You are to design the initiative that they might use to proceed, identifying the main sub-targets and adding any you feel will be relevant. Note any difficulties that you encounter as you proceed through the process, and make sure that the outcome is a coherent and workable system in four ways:

1. The visual reference that staff could follow.
2. The management routes that are identified for the ongoing interventions during the project.
3. The targets that are set.
4. The critical questions you feel are relevant, and how you will explore these with all staff.

Some considerations

1. Point out the potential and the payoffs: Make sure that staff have ample opportunity to explore and talk about the potential benefits of the activity that will be engaged in. Help them to understand and to experience the value of self-evaluation against the targets as well as feeding back into the school-wide reviews.

2.   *Keep it small at the start:*   Do not be drawn into huge changes. Find out how the organisation learns best. Do this through open discussion. Engage with staff in a learning process, ask their opinions, inquire into what is working for them as they make changes.

3.   *Keep it simple:*   It does not have to be immensely complex. Clear thinking and appropriate techniques are invaluable. Find out what is working and why it is working. Refine and personalise externally relevant techniques to fit your set-up.

4.   *Incorporate it:*   Make the process of target setting and monitoring a central process to the operation of the school and to individuals. There is no reason why the process cannot be linked throughout the school operation into curriculum approaches and assessment as well as school-wide change.

5.   *Make it useful:*   Learn as a team to report when it is working so that others can consider applying to their own situations. Make the changes matter – ensure that they are important to many people and reflect a real need.

6.   *Clarify the criteria of success:*   Be clear and encourage colleagues to be clear about what you are trying to do. Be alert for new ways in which clarity can be built in. This might include imagery, mapping, models – whatever works well for the team.

7.   *Identify and use strengths:*   Nothing is more demoralising than to have a fine set of targets without the possibility of ever getting there. Be realistic. Build on your staff strengths and use them to full advantage through blending of teams so that they can learn from each other and develop skills for the other 'future' projects. Plan in what will be needed next to take the team forward. Explore with them the necessary components so that they can search out appropriate resources, courses and materials to assist them in their activity and learning.

8.   *Encourage creativity:*   To have diversity is not a weakness. It indicates that there is a strong-willed group who know that to learn is to diversify. Encourage diversity of approaches. Listen to other and conflicting viewpoints and approaches to your own and learn and examine why they work for other people. Act on what you learn. Is it relevant to your setting? How will you know?

9.   *Place self-learning and target setting as a high profile event:* Make sure that each staff member has the opportunity to develop

personally and has the chance to work frequently with others, to meet and to read. Make sure that the work they do in this area is respected and valued, not ignored or seen as a threat or devalued by constant mocking. Self-learning is a huge commitment so let it pay off for the organisation as well as the individual. Do not miss out on making the links and celebrating the strengths that this will bring to the school.

3 Learning through teams

Introduction

In this chapter we explore what approaches might be taken to establish and sustain a successful team. To begin with we will explore what is meant by a team. We will then proceed to look at profiles of personnel and seek strengths and areas for development of the individual. We will then look at evidence of previous strategies of team learning, which can be used as a base upon which to introduce new ways of working. We will describe learning routes which can successfully be shared and used with staff to develop their internal understanding of their role in a team.

What is a team?

What images come to mind when you hear the word team?

- List them.
- Classify your list.
- What are the teams best linked to? To sport, music, television, politics, industry, education?

Teams are a feature of social life. They exist in the glamorous and the mundane. We live in various groupings that we call family and those groupings are to a greater or lesser extent team reliant with people taking roles and trusting others to do so as well. Teams are emotional, social and more functional communities of people, but they can just as easily be dysfunctional. Likewise the team in a school. What works as a team in one school setting might not transfer into a different school setting or work as successfully.

There are some very simple characteristics of team building:

- working together and applying the very human characteristic of belief in each other,
- patience with each other's failures,
- trust that we can get better at it,
- working hard at improving communication,
- better undertaking daily tasks together,
- establishing strong relationships,
- sharing an appreciation of each other's viewpoint or preferred way of working.

The first part of this chapter describes the types of team that might be the ideal, and how to create the appropriate strength of blend of persons. We will examine how team building can be a feature of the development of the school operation integrated into staff meetings and core activity that involves all people.

We will then consider team learning. This is altogether different. It is possibly the most challenging and demanding aspect of school improvement. The process is emotional, intellectual, spiritual, micro-political and social. It is also an unfamiliar aspect of school life. We tend to have our own classes, we teach in our own idiosyncratic ways, we meet to discuss policies and practices. But does this constitute team *learning*.

Team learning begins from self-knowledge. It involves establishing approaches that enable you to create knowledge of and alignment with colleagues in the team, and then it means progressing with an awareness of that knowledge.

- Think of the last time that you sat in a meeting and you really wanted to say something but did not say it because you were worried that it might be misunderstood, misconstrued or would cause embarrassment.
- Think how you felt at the time.
- Think what might have happened if you had intervened and said what you felt was important.

Teams that are unfamiliar with learning techniques frequently collude to 'cloak' (Smith & Keith, 1971) or to hide important issues from each other. This is the essence of not learning together because in doing it, we openly engage in actions that fail to create stronger links. This chapter will describe ways of making team learning a natural activity in school which can establish ways of working that facilitate deep levels of team practice that enables the team to learn together about their approaches to the job, and their areas of personal and collective need.

What are the characteristics of a learning team?

The core skills of a learning team are:

- trust,
- inquiry skills,
- reflective skills.

Trust implies that people genuinely believe in each other's abilities and the potential of their ability to help each other and improve what they are doing for mutual benefit. *Inquiry skills* aim to find out what is happening and how it is happening to inform the building of that trust. *Reflective skills* aim to examine what has been found and to explore the best ways that the people in the team can communicate the findings to all.

Team learning creates its own rules

A team that intends to work closely together for any period of time will establish its own rules. These will develop as a result of the governing values and purposes that are held in common. Whenever people get into situations where they might be faced with a threat or embarrassment, they are more than likely to act in ways that bypass the threat or embarrassment and undertake action to cover it up. Because this is the case in most individuals, and most individuals will use these actions, they become a part of the way in which teams establish ways of working. The actions themselves start to be seen as the right way to go about doing things; they are sensible, appropriate and practical ways of doing things.

An organisation, made up of alliances of different teams, will begin to develop characteristic defensive routines, and these protect people from particular ways of working, but they also inhibit the opportunity to see situations differently.

To overcome defences of this sort can be very difficult. However, there are ways in which it can happen. In particular we can explore with teams the 'undiscussables' (Argyris, 1990), the 'things which we don't talk about'. We can begin to discuss 'why we don't talk about these things.' Ways to overcome these include:

- telling the truth in the best way that the person knows it,

- bringing information to the attention of the group immediately,
- talking about the issues and not the personalities,
- not pointing the finger,
- not assuming that other people know how decisions will be made and kept to,
- how it will deal with violations to the rules.

Establish the team operating rules and then stick to them but make sure that people have an opportunity to reflect on the rules frequently and where necessary to promote discussion to ensure their modification.

The rules might appear to be deterministic. However, they are vital to facilitating learning together. They enable people to participate and to build safe areas into what can otherwise be threatening and difficult territory. The implications of not having a rule system to base team learning on is that people will not engage fully because they will fear the consequences – they will not generate trust. That is why it is equally important that review on a regular basis takes place on these rules themselves. People will then have a voice in the process of the team decision making.

Team learning demands advocacy and inquiry

The ability to engage in dialogue is not something that we do very success-fully. As was recently heard at a training session, 'the Government tells the LEA, the LEA tells the head, the head tells the teacher, and the teacher tells the kids.'

With this background noise, we are conscious that the suggestion to establish a programme in school that actively encourages opportunity to *talk* and *listen* and *think together* may not be a welcome addition. We suggest that it should function *instead* of present practices.

The process of talking and listening

Becoming aware of the development of dialogue requires a language *about* the language of discussion. It enables staff to reflect constructively on team development as they move through different levels of appreciation of their work together. Figure 3.1 indicates the ways in which a discussion might flow.

Ways of fostering dialogue

You can't manufacture dialogue. Dialogue requires that people know what they are getting into, and it demands that they are frequently thinking

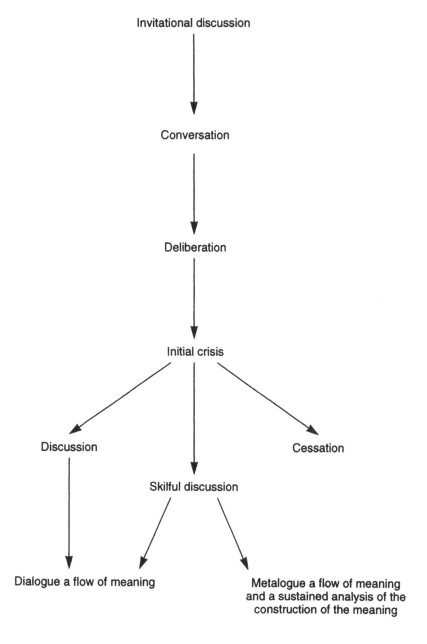

Figure 3.1   Discourse process

through the implications of the dialogue on the actions they do later.

The best way to begin might be to link the process to something that is due to happen in school.

This activity is simple. It establishes a link directly between staff development and student learning.

Process: Two teachers who feel comfortable working together discuss an aspect of their work in class or within school that they wish to improve or that they have already been involved in and which they now want to reflect more purposefully upon. They can use the questions in Figure 3.2 to focus their discussion.

The teachers need to spend about 30 minutes talking through the issues they have raised. The outcome of the talk is to establish a set of reference points which they feel are important ones to share with colleagues. These are then reported back to the staff as a whole, and matters arising are identified.

Team learning through peer tutoring

A second method which facilitates internal discussion and team learning is to work as a tutoring pair.

Two staff who feel comfortable working in each other's classrooms spend time together defining the focus for the involvement. The intention is that the agenda is defined by teacher 1 who will receive the other teacher 2 into class. The other teacher is responsible for defining the specific aspects of guidance which the first teacher wishes to receive.

They then go into class, and teacher 2 observes teacher 1 in the lesson. Teachers 1 and 2 then proceed to reflect together on the work that took place, specific to the agenda that was set by teacher 1. The outcome can be to continue, to recommend new ways of approaching the task and repeating the session, to report to the whole school, or to move on to new areas of work or pursue it further in class or through other forms of study.

Learning routes

These two examples of simple strategic discussion and action offer opportunities for individual staff members to develop new learning. They can, when carefully constructed, initiate team learning through the range of activity that will be discussed, the type of approaches taken, and the aspects of the work which other colleagues in the team might have done differently. In each of these scenarios, there is therefore a vast untapped potential for growth.

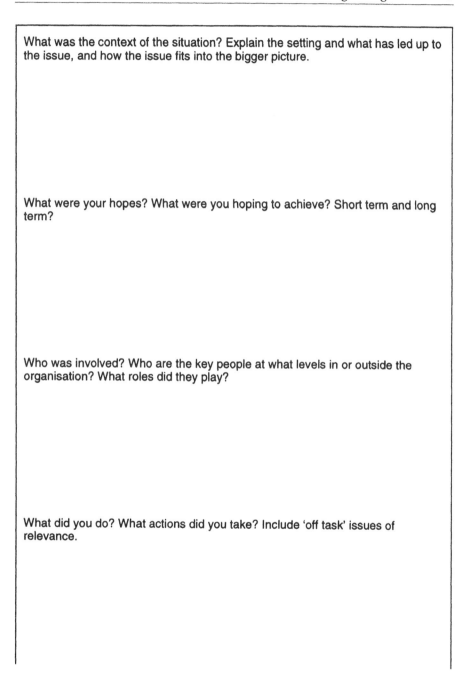

What was the context of the situation? Explain the setting and what has led up to the issue, and how the issue fits into the bigger picture.

What were your hopes? What were you hoping to achieve? Short term and long term?

Who was involved? Who are the key people at what levels in or outside the organisation? What roles did they play?

What did you do? What actions did you take? Include 'off task' issues of relevance.

Figure 3.2   A structured discussion

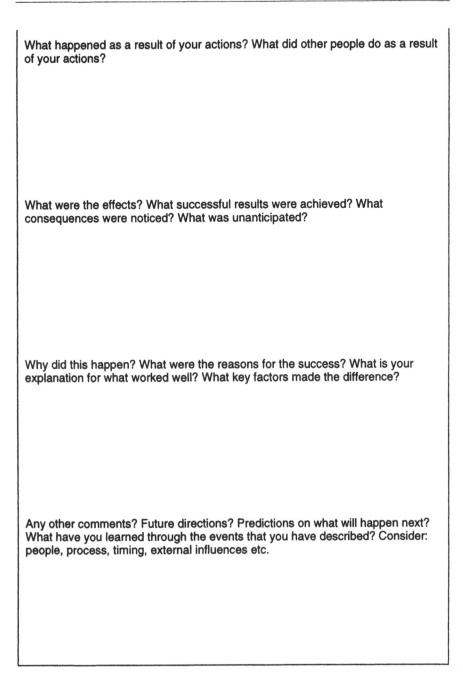

What happened as a result of your actions? What did other people do as a result of your actions?

What were the effects? What successful results were achieved? What consequences were noticed? What was unanticipated?

Why did this happen? What were the reasons for the success? What is your explanation for what worked well? What key factors made the difference?

Any other comments? Future directions? Predictions on what will happen next? What have you learned through the events that you have described? Consider: people, process, timing, external influences etc.

Figure 3.2   *concluded*

Creating teams and maintaining teams through the sustained generation of ideas

Teams will function if they have a function. This implies that we can maintain teams if challenges are placed in front of them which demand collective activity.

We know that everyone is creative, resourceful and can come up with solutions to problems. There is no doubt of this because to not do so is not to be alive and to have survived through to adulthood. What is useful to remember with teams is that they are going to represent a variety of perspectives on any given problem. This is at once useful – because it will open out a range of possible approaches in response to the problem – and a hindrance, because it can promote conflict.

Our school system does not facilitate team building. It does not create the right climate for team development because it rewards individual achievement and therefore enhances the status of doing things by one's self. Teamwork requires co-operative relationships at all levels of the school and this in itself challenges the contemporary hierarchical management paradigm.

What makes a team creative and successful?

The characteristics of a creative team arise often from the roles and responsibilities that individual members feel comfortable with inside the team. However, there are some pointers (Figure 3.3) we might use to identify attributes of team success (Lumsdaine and Lumsdaine, 1995).

Reflect on the list in the team that you work with most. To what extent does it represent your team? Where do you feel there is scope for growth?

Contributing factors

Time is a factor in teams becoming effective together. Initially, the people in a team will continue to act as individuals. The catalyst for drawing a team together is the focus upon some common goals to which each person will have a responsibility to the other. Equally important, once efforts begin to try and achieve the goals, is the recognition of the effort – the journey as well as the outcome therefore comes into play as part of the means of consolidating group activity.

One very useful technique we have used frequently with teams in the process of consolidation is to introduce a simple structure which can then be visited frequently as the team begins to learn more about the way in which it is operating.

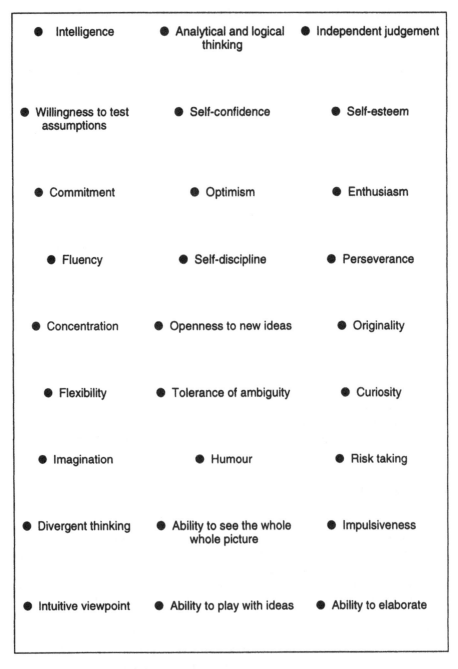

Figure 3.3   Attributes of creative teams

Substitute? Who else instead? What else instead? Other place? Other time? Other ingredient? Material? Other process? Other approach?

Combine? How about blends? Assortments? Combining purposes? Combining units? Combining ideas? Combining functions?

Adapt? What else is like this? What other ideas does this suggest? Any idea in the past that could be copied or adapted?

Modify? Change the meaning, colour, motion, sound, taste, form, shape? Other changes? New twist?

Magnify? Add? Greater frequency? Stronger? Larger? Higher? Longer? Multiply? Exaggerate?

Minimise? What might we subtract? Eliminate? Smaller? Lighter? Slower? Split? Less frequent? Condense? Streamline?

Put to other uses? New ways to use the object/issue as it is? Other uses if modified?

Eliminate? What to remove? Edit? In order to create extra space for new issues?

Rearrange? Other layout? Sequence? Pace change? Other pattern? Schedule change? Transpose cause and effect?

Reverse? Opposites? Turn it backward? Upside down? Inside out? Mirror it? Transpose the positive with the negative?

Figure 3.4 SCAMPER
Source: Osborn, 1963.

This technique prompts a series of 'starters' which can be applied to situations that a team has to respond to, using the acrostic **SCAMPER** (see Figure 3.4):

Substitute
Combine
Adapt
Modify – Magnify – Minimise
Put to other uses
Eliminate
Rearrange – Reverse capturing the essence of the activity.

In effect, what we are suggesting is that a simple way of developing a team is to pose a 'What if?' and a 'What else?' question. As long as these questions have a purpose and are not contrived, the team will respond.

A significant part of establishing a purpose is establishing, as the existing rather than the desired state for the team, the possibility of change, and the possibility that the staff team will be active agents in a changed situation. In this situation, the team will learn. They will also be modelling the types of inquiry which they would likely desire from students. Exploration can then continue through to the classroom level where further connections between the organisational and the personal level can be established.

4 Thinking systems in school communities

The school is a fascinating community which can be thought of as a system. This implies that there will be ways of operating which the school will take as given, and which underpin many of the day-to-day ways of working within the school community. The consequent activity within the school is to a great extent governed by the rules, be they overt or covert, that the system dictates. These can be as simple as the way a letter is processed through the school, to the complex array of interlinking issues that come together within the system to enable a change to happen and to last.

The consideration of the way that the school community functions as a system, and the way it inhibits or facilitates successful and effective ways of operating, is an important part of the leadership role. Leaders need to be able to reflect on the nature of the system so as to be in a position, if the need arises, to introduce ways of working that will reconfigure the approaches that the system takes.

Systems thinking assumes that the system of the school has identifiable and recurring patterns and that real change will be more likely to come about through reforms to the system rather than directly through 'fixing' the people. Systems thinking assumes that staff within the school will focus their collective attention upon the central causes of action in school and on long-term consequences of such causes, rather than just dealing with the immediacy of quick fixes. To think in such a way is to search for the complex in any situation. To examine what is understood about the dynamics within the day-to-day work as well as being sustained by a belief that there will be patterns and common principles which will be observable in whatever we do within the system of the school.

The systems thinking approach to school development does not assume that such patterns are obvious, nor does it mean that they are all able to be easily worked out. What it does mean is that in school there will be continual changes in the ebbs and flows of understanding and discovery of the way the school functions as a community across the range of individuals and staff as a whole. The advantage gained by systems thinking is the ability to think holistically and not partially about the nature and process of change. If we fail to engage in systems thinking we run the great risk of ending up in stringing projects together, never profoundly affecting change, and frequently feeling that circumstances are taking us over. The impact of not engaging in systems thinking is in feeling that one is being governed all the time by circumstances beyond any possibility of control – the system is a powerful dynamic, and we delude ourselves that we are able to maintain total control. We can however make more informed responses as a result of a better understanding of the system in which we work. As leaders we ignore it at our peril.

Systems thinking implies a few basic concepts

Systems thinking is perhaps best described in anthropological terms: 'making the ordinary extraordinary'. When we apply such a notion to school this implies that we engage in a series of simple concepts about the school and how we perceive its operation from a personal perspective and from an organisational perspective.

Each of these concepts is described and techniques are considered which can facilitate school activity which relates to them.

Seeing change as a process and not an event

Think about school development in terms of it being a process and not a set of clearly defined events. Because we engage as players in that process through our considered actions, we have a direct part to play in the shaping of that process and therefore in the development of the system in which we operate.

That we strive to understand better the system in which we operate

Systems are perceived things whose elements 'hold together' and continually interact with each other as they move towards common purposes.

There are no correct answers

There is never a single correct answer within a system because there are always going to be dynamics within that offer the scope and the potential for alternative explanations.

An example might be a staff meeting. You plan a clear strategy to achieve a policy goal. You present this in conjunction with the relevant staff to other members of the school team, and you can foresee some likely difficulties and forecast for them. However, there will be other issues which come up that were not expected and were as powerful in their influence upon the debate. What do you do with this situation?

Assuming a single response implies a linear form of thinking. Although this allows us to sequence out our understanding of a situation, such thinking often fails to accommodate the different and varied dimensions of any problem. Therefore our approach in systems thinking is to widen the potential for alternative explanations and dimensions of response to a given situation.

As Figure 4.1 indicates, systems thinking demands different methodological approaches which incorporate diverse sources of data and then attempt to construct meaning derived from the analysis of these data. All the time, it is vital to maintain the whole rather than the partial view.

Systems are very resistant to being divided into parts

As the system has many embedded features which will have an effect on what we do, regardless of what we may wish to do, there will be considerable time lapses and intermediate actions and events as change unfolds in ways that we have planned for. The most prevalent of the factors which influence the system is the school's underlying culture.

Traditionally in school development activity the approach was to atomise the organisation into constituent parts and to assume that we maintain a sense of togetherness in the organisation as we did this. The development planning process is an example of such an approach. There are many aspects of school development undertaken but critically, these often fail to weave together sufficiently coherently to maintain an overall sense of direction and purpose. Rather, different tasks are undertaken or delegated to different staff members before enough time is spent considering the reasons for the tasks, the likely effects, the other ways that the goals that define the tasks might be

PROBLEM:	PROBLEM:
linear response model	non-linear response model
response identification	issue analysis
response synthesis	initial responses
response approach	alternative responses
response strategy	initial identification of root causes
actions	synthesis of responses
observation of impact	responses
	identification of the location of these responses into wider school developments
	intermediate action
	review
	replanning
	main actions and waiting time with further intermediate events/actions
	observation of impact – direct and indirect on school structure and school culture

Figure 4.1   Problem definition

achieved and so on. Furthermore, there has been an assumption at a later stage that the atomisation enables staff to reconstruct a sense of wholeness of an issue merely by reporting back the effect of each of the separate sets of activities of the subject co-ordinators.

Such thinking causes problems, because it makes the school as an organisation legitimise the breaking down of the purposes it undertakes as the responsibility of named people rather than maintaining a collective sense of responsibility for change. The outcome of this is that blame at a later stage is located on people, although it is the system that has been created that is often the cause of the fault and not the people.

Systems thinking draws attention to the profound problems that atomising an organisation causes – namely, that by doing one focused and delegated task, one can easily lose sight of the target and instead end up focusing on a multiplicity of sub-goals linked to a personal task, but failing to connect across from these goals to other ones that colleagues may have that are compatible. A principle of systems thinking is to pursue detail of those sub-goals and the dynamics of a larger problem by maintaining an overview of the initiative. The reason for this is that we cannot afford areas of the school to be off-limits; we cannot think that there will not be an effect in some other part of school just because it isn't planned or predetermined into the sub-goals, or because it is part of some undiscussable aspect of the way the school works as a system.

One way of overcoming this profoundly difficult effect of organisational leadership is to interlink the co-ordination roles. This is so that different subject disciplines have an overlapping co-ordination role. The school thereby initiates into its structure a set of activities which are bound together more coherently and fosters connections beginning to be made by the staff as they undertake their roles.

- Reflect on the system in your school.
- What aspects of school life do you simply take for granted?
- To what extent does taking this for granted inhibit the opportunity for the school community to change purposefully?
- How can you constructively create situations where staff are taking an integrated approach to their work, rather than one that atomises the necessary work of the school into component elements?

Interdependence of the system components – leading staff towards wide-angle viewing

A useful component to the thinking on systems thinking is to bear in mind the interdependence of all things across the school community. This facilitates a wide-angle view of development, and presupposes a staff culture which embraces change more readily because it appreciates the dimensions which can arise from any problem. Such a staff culture takes time to establish and would be likely to convey many of the learning principles suggested by Moore (1988, in Stoll and Fink, 1996, p.154):

- to be collaborative, involving participants in diagnosing needs, decision making, designing, implementing and evaluating staff development,
- to help learners achieve self-direction and be enabled to define their own objectives using professional content to meet their needs,
- to capitalise on learners' experiences, using them as a starting point,
- to foster participation, with learners helping to decide learning methods and structure the learning environment,
- to cultivate critical thinking as reflective thinking helping learners examine cultural and organisational assumptions as well as for their own practice,
- to foster learning for action, with opportunities for decision making and strategy planning,
- to encourage problem posing and problem solving, as closely connected as possible to learners' real problems.

This culture is active in the sourcing out of processes that allow greater meaning to be made of the change process and the way that the school operates at the classroom, school and community level. The active seeking of connections and approaches which can facilitate such practice is central to systems thinking, and crucial to the leader, in the form of headteacher, and the staff in the form of teachers leading initiatives and seeking integrated support with colleagues.

Cause and effect

Our actions might not emerge in the form of outcomes 'where' we predict – 'how' we predict – or 'when' we predict.

The assumption of a simple cause and effect in school development is a false one. Keep looking for the root sources of the problems that are being focused upon and which are being tried to be solved. There are often opportunities for substantial leverage in the development of the school in quite unexpected places.

Ask staff to reflect on the positive and the negative implications of an issue using the graphic tool (in Figure 4.2) by locating the issue in the centre and working outwards from the initial issue identifying the different possible features of the issue under scrutiny.

The graphic illustrates that there will be positives or 'good things' to come

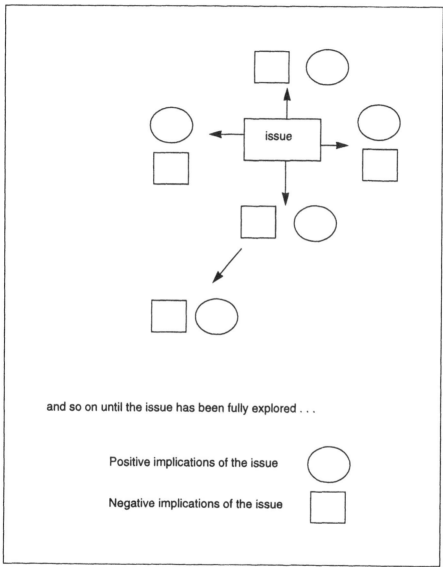

Figure 4.2   Open issue analysis

from the intervention but that there will also be negative aspects which can be considered or, more often and more sadly, are likely to be ignored. By making a point of identifying the negative implications of the event or issue, it is possible to consider the likely effect of such reactions and where necessary modify our work. A further advantage in developing forecasting in this way is that it begins to provide material that enables other initiatives to link in to it. The graphic prompts detailed thinking beyond the immediate ramifications of an event into the likely future effect of it. Staff begin to identify opportunities through which they can locate changes in the wider development of the school to the issue under direct focus and in this way the collective meaning of the change is better appreciated by those engaged in the change.

Using positive and negative stimuli for forecasting change

You recognise that the staff within your school are able to make links between the positive effects of change and the likely difficulties. Staff can recognise the fact that much of the development plan is unpredictable but that they can move within such unpredictability and can respond where necessary. This is a reassuring and confidence-boosting recognition. As with other aspects of systems thinking, use the realisation to good effect by seeking staff insights into other aspects of school life where the unpredictability/predictability issue is prominent. The thinking that has emerged from the forecasting of development planning identifies a way forward which notices benefits and pitfalls. To develop this technique we now try to form some simple classifications of the problem through which our systems thinking can be further developed. The locating of the problems helps to particularise the change into the wider developments that the school is attempting.

What type of problem are we confronting here?

System-based problems refer to the complex mix of factors that make up the situation that is under scrutiny. In studying an issue or problem we frequently make reference to the fact that other impacting factors *may and probably will* be operating.

Having made an initial location of the problem we further classify into two system types:

Type 1:   'simple problems'
Type 2:   'complex problems'.

Figure 4.3 points to the distinction that has been drawn between the two forms of problems.

Simple problems	Complex problems
small number of elements	a large number of elements
few interactions between elements	many interactions between the elements
attributes of the elements are predetermined	attributes of the elements are not predetermined
interaction between the elements is highly organised	interactions between elements is loosely organised
well defined procedures govern their behaviour	they are probabilistic in their behaviour
the system does not evolve in time	the system evolves over time
sub-systems do not pursue own goals	sub-systems are purposeful and generate their own goals
the system remains unaffected by behavioural influences	the system is subject to behavioural influences
the system is largely closed to the environment	the system is largely open to the environment

Figure 4.3   Simple and complex problem construction

Look at a key problem in school.

- What is the source of the problem: internal or external?
- Is the problem complex or simple in its present form?
- How would you most obviously solve or respond to the problem?
- What would be your typical strategic response to this issue?

Now source out three less direct routes which still seem to address the problem.

You might want to involve more people from outside the frequently consulted group. You might want to look at the initiative in a different timescale, or you might consider relocating the problem to a different discussion meeting that can link it to a curriculum activity or another school development. However you proceed, try and introduce something new into the approach that has not previously featured as part of your modelling of this type of problem before.

What insights does this bring to your initial approach? How might each of the three new approaches be drawn upon in the actions which you might undertake now in response to the root problem?

Widening the analysis can liberate thinking very effectively to enable a range of different approaches to occur (see Figure 4.4).

System approaches take time

The central lesson of substantive development is the need to enjoy the moment as well as the achievement of getting there. Expect time delays, expect problems, and take full advantage of them as sources of new data with which you can inform the ongoing development of the work.

Have an ear for the quiet whisperings of development

Often great ideas go unheard because everyone is so focused on solving the immediate problem that they fail to hear the voices of the people who are gaining new insights as they proceed on the developmental journey. The systems approach demands that we pay attention to more than the obvious. We are on the look out for material that informs and provides new insights into the ways that we currently do things. We could draw on the anthropological perspective to inform such action where 'making the ordinary appear extraordinary' is the foundation of the practice.

A system encompasses the features described here and many other features. If we bear these in mind as we consider our work in school then we have a deeper range of opportunities for development and growth. A growing awareness of our ability to understand the system will be evidenced

What type of a problem is this?	simple	complex
Why?		
How would you normally respond to this problem?		
List some typical strategic responses to this type of problem	a) b) c) d)	
Suggest three other routes to explore in response to the problem	1. 2. 3.	
Insights and inferences gained from the investigation are:		
Further action is therefore needed in:		

Figure 4.4   Problem analysis

through a deeper appreciation of those internal system indicators that the school has that are particular to the way the school functions. These often come from established activity embedded into an 'organisational psyche' more than that of individuals because they are part of the collective expectation of the school. This is something which takes time to learn and even longer to change, should we feel that change is needed.

Systems thinking therefore accommodates the ideas that are particular to one school site, but which we can see in evidence over many different sites:

- a pre-existing social structure is always there before we ever begin to try and introduce a change,
- all parts of the system are interconnected,
- the system will resist change in fundamental and powerful ways,
- while each system is unique they share attributes that are common across many other school sites.

What metaphors would you use to describe your school system?

- What does the metaphor say about the way in which you perceive its functions and its methods?
- How does the school go about making important decisions?
- How does the school communicate as a system?
- How does the school invite the participation of its members to share and collectively develop?
- Is it a healthy system or is it one that needs nurturing back to good health?
- If you were to change the metaphor, how might this help you to think differently about the way that the school could function?

Systems thinking facilitates a better vision

Systems thinking enables us to develop strategic approaches that 'see the forest as well as the trees' (Senge, 1990). Such thinking demands that we work with and involve different groups of people, different decision making processes, putting different procedures and structures in place and seeking to make these interlock and affect each other, sometimes in planned ways, and sometimes in unplanned and predicted ways. Systems possess powerful drives towards steadiness and therefore actively resist change, therefore changing complex systems, such as schools, demands first an understanding of how the system works and then how they can be changed.

Make a list of those aspects of school performance which are most resistant to change.

- What distinguishes these from the readily changeable parts of school?
- What positive lessons can be learnt from the first and second lists?
- How can these be applied to the introduction of future developments in school?

School can now be looked at as a series of inter-related elements, which can be used as data to inform systems thinking.

Identifying a problem situation

Identify a problem that you are familiar with. Spend a few minutes reflecting on this problem and then write down what you feel are the core components of the problem.

This problem needs to be important to you and to the school. It should be something that you really want to try and understand and something that matters to you.

If you find that you are having trouble limiting the problem to a couple of sentences, try and refocus. Talk to a colleague about the problem and tune down the scope of the issue you are dealing with. It will be easy to expand the problem up again later.

Try to make it a problem that has something of a history which you are in a position to be able to describe.

Be accurate. There is always a tendency to want to play down some of the really difficult or problematic aspects of the issue you are describing. Do not fall into the trap of avoidance because the problem will be skewed and later efforts to make a difference to the situation will be based on misinformation.

Systems thinking is about discovery, synthesis, analysis, diagnosis and, importantly, intuition. Although it is necessary to stick to the facts and to evidence, do not be afraid to say what you feel to be significant, even if at this point you are not sure why it might be so. These insights can often illuminate a problem and make others reconsider and redesign their viewpoint so encourage the exploration of how people 'feel' about the problem.

Avoid jumping to solutions and conclusions. We do not know yet what the likely best response is to be. Not jumping to a conclusion is part of the discipline in the process of systems thinking.

Map out all of the quick fixes that you see that lead directly from the problem situation

Some aspects of the problem will obviously lead you in well proven directions. Instead of just taking that route on auto-pilot, make a deliberate recorded process map of the route to solve the problem. Make this visible. It is something that you and your colleagues are going to add to later. Don't be afraid to put the obvious. It might be obvious to you but that does not guarantee it will be for others. Similarly, ask the same of your colleagues. They will see things that you will not and doing so will illuminate the thinking that you are applying and offer others the opportunity to tap into the initiative.

Identify the undesirable impacts

Having made as comprehensive a set of responses to the fixes as you can at this time, now revisit the issue and highlight the undesirable impacts – the areas that you perhaps are unwilling to go down and the areas that seem to be irrelevant implications of the responses. Explore each one carefully and ask whether these are in fact useful additions. Try to provide some basis or rationale for the elimination of these responses from the final approach to the problem that you might make.

A useful question here might be: can we do without this approach in response to the problem here?

Identify fundamental solutions

What is left? Having undergone a series of trawls through the response that you have made as a team, you will have a limited number of more fundamental solutions to the issue that you are tackling.

From this base position the next step is to consider the system implications. In each of the following question areas bear in mind that they are not isolated issues. They will link with each other, and probably with features of the school development that are outside the remit of the direct work.

Areas to reflect upon which facilitate the thinking on the system

The central area of concern in systems thinking is the growth and movement of the system over time. The catalyst of such growth and movement is a change; planned or unplanned, it will impact in many ways upon the school system. Therefore to concern oneself as a leader with the change process and understanding the impact of the change process upon the school as a system is an important part of leadership.

The purpose of the next section is to reflect on some of the significant features of the leadership role.

The change process and the impact upon individuals

- How will this change affect the individual members of the team?
- What considerations are necessary to facilitate their involvement and commitment to the initiative?
- What learning attributes might be usefully employed to involve and prompt widespread team involvement?

To investigate these areas it might be useful to employ analysis of the levels of concern that the staff are expressing. One proven model that usefully enables development activity to be pursued on evaluation of response is the Concerns Based Adoption Model or CBAM model (Loucks and Hall, 1979). In the CBAM model there are seven identified stages of concern (see Figure 4.5) which can be referred to by staff and through which it is then possible to identify the profile of response to the initiative. This opens up the opportunity for staff to explore personally and collectively the sense of engagement with the change. It can lead to a deeper level of examination of the likely result of the change if it were to proceed given the present levels of concern, so it is a most valuable instrument to gauge opinion.

Warning! It is well worth remembering that it is only an instrument to assist the formulation of your own viewpoint. The danger of this, like any other device which gathers a particular form of data, is that we then invest too much meaning in the findings and we lose sight of the whole issue. So explore the findings, but maintain the critical mindset.

CBAM is a method of analysis that enables consistent attention to be placed against the change and its staff level impact.

From CBAM we have frequently found the table illustrated in Figure 4.6 a useful locating device. It allows staff to then discuss together the implications of the change from the personal level. Bear in mind here that this approach opens the personal response to group scrutiny. It has to be done therefore only in situations where staff will feel comfortable with such approaches.

This device can be used either by referring to each teacher response, or by not requesting personal response via name, but by requesting response openly the staff can at least gain an insight into the implications of the initiative and the present feelings about it.

In a similar manner to CBAM, Clarke and Christie (1996) have used a simple typology with teachers to address the feeling at staff level of an improvement effort. This typology draws upon five typical responses by staff to any initiative (see Figure 4.7).

The response types can be located on a matrix and staff can log their response to the change at any time in the process of implementation. The

CBAM Stages of concern	Expressions of concern	Intervention example
6 Refocusing	I have some ideas about ways to make it work even better.	
5 Collaboration	I am concerned about relating what I am doing with what other instructors are doing.	Team planning
4 Consequence	I want to know how my using this approach will affect my students.	Analyse student performance. Observer provides feedback
3 Management	I seem to be spending all my time in getting material ready.	Observe/talk with teachers who are not experiencing difficulty
2 Personal	I want to know how my using this approach will affect me.	One-on-one conversations
1 Informational	I would like to know more about it.	Awareness sessions
0 Awareness	I am not concerned about it (the innovation).	Announcements Meetings

Figure 4.5   Concerns Based Adoption Model (CBAM)

CBAM Stages of concern	Teacher name	Teacher name	Teacher name	Teacher name	Teacher name	Teacher name
6 Refocusing						
5 Collaboration						
4 Consequence						
3 Management						
2 Personal						
1 Informational						
0 Awareness						

Figure 4.6 Matrix of responses to person

outcome information provides a useful frame of discussion and provides an evaluative tool for staff to look at the movement over time of staff response to an initiative (see Figure 4.8).

The mapping of responses in this way illuminates the dynamics of the school culture in any initiative and indicates that any improvement agenda will have a range of possible directions and a similar range of possible implications related to staff response. If these dimensions are not taken into account then the long-term intentions of the initiative can be drawn into question because the likelihood of embedding into the school culture

Response type	Description
Reactive	This change is of no use to me because . . .
Engaging	This change might be of some use so I will . . .
Active	This change is of use and I'll get involved by . . .
Reflective	How has this change been of use to me?
Creative	Now that we know how useful this change can be, we intend to . . .

Figure 4.7 Response types

through shared actions, beliefs and values is being ignored at the expense of short-term structural expediency.

Alongside such personnel implications, we might draw upon five simple principles of human learning (NSDC, 1995). This enables us to locate where the attention might be placed in response to our findings from the CBAM of mapping response activity.

1. We should promote our professional development from a proven

Proposed
development: . . . . date . . . /. . . / . . .
Meeting issue related to the development:

. . . .
. . . .
. . . .
. . . .

Recorded staff response profile

Response type	teacher A	teacher B	teacher C	teacher D
reactive				
engaging				
active				
reflective				
creative				

Figure 4.8   Response sheet

Discussion points raised as a result of these responses:

Implications for next steps in the development:

Staff based:

Initiative based:

Timescale: term   term   term

Figure 4.8   *concluded*

knowledge base. Motivation for growth and learning comes from interest and self worth. We need to foster these qualities in all of the work we undertake in staff development.

2. Staff development must enhance staff confidence so that they feel able to be successful at the job of teaching.
3. There are benefits of interdependence and collaboration.
4. There is an imperative to develop staff development outcomes. Staff need to know the level of importance, expected outcomes and rationale for changes in their work to ensure positive results.
5. Success will take time, resources and supporting structures. The systems-thinking leader will be conscious of such needs and be eager to grasp opportunities to locate development in recognisable aspects of the organisation and its staff development (NSDC, 1995, p17).

What are the organisational implications of the initiative?

Realistically, can a change be undertaken in the timescale that you have established? Remember that a good rule of thumb on planning of this type is to think of the amount of time it will take and double it!

What sources of data are going to be essential for the initiative to be informed and validated at a later stage?

These data might be drawn from a wide range of sources: individual responses, team responses to the initiative, teacher assessment, standard assessment tasks and other standardised data leading to information on pupil performance, questionnaire responses from pupils, parents and other stakeholders in school, as well as informal sources of information.

QUESTION: What is the most suitable form of staff development that can be taken to facilitate and inform the team of the process and intended outcomes of the response to the problem situation?

This is very much context dependent. However, there are some practical routes through systems thinking initiatives which can be productively informative of both the process of development and of the intended outcomes in response to a situation.

Informing on the process of change

We have already talked in Chapter 2 of the timeline technique that can identify essential components of the change activity. This technique usefully informs on structural dimensions of the change. We can add to this a well explored route of questionnaire and analysis of response to this timeline technique and build up a useful data source which enhances staff appreciation of the nature of the change process.

Some of our recent work (Clarke, forthcoming) has incorporated focused questionnaires with timeline methods (see Figure 4.9). These take the form of discussions with staff on their attitude to the process of school change, its impact on morale, on teacher confidence and on following the desired pace that staff would wish to proceed with the initiative. We have observed that staff find the activity valuable because they are in a better position to re-examine their own expectations and hopes that emerge from the change that is being proposed.

These items ask you to think about the improvement initiative in which you are involved, with respect to four 'domains of application'.

Please circle the statements in the following manner:

1. those that best reflect your view about the process so far (in colour A),
2. those that best reflect your view of the school staff as a whole of the process so far (colour B).

The approach is used in two different but complementary ways:

1. The staff are asked to respond personally to the statements on the sheet.
2. They are then asked to locate where they feel that their staff colleagues would place themselves as a whole school in regard of the development.

The outcome data are discussed and used as material to evaluate the present impact of the development and the areas where staff are indicating that they personally and collectively need support.

For example: a staff response might indicate on the 'linking ideas on the process' domain that they have an 'active' response to the process. This would locate the necessary staff development upon the development of an effective response. This implies work needed on inter-linking activity to process.

Other responses can be viewed in a similar manner. The important issue is the support areas that can be identified and the differentiation between staff response which can at times be wide ranging. The wider the range of staff personal response to whole staff perceived response, the greater the need to address the earlier stages of development of process awareness.

Reflect on where you would locate your own responses on the chart. What do you find that informs you of your perception of the change process taking place in school?

	minimal	engaged	active	effective	reflective/ creative
linking ideas on the process	– a few links in the development are established – single forms of analysis are being made	– we are making multiple connections – we are providing limited supporting detail	– we are able to establish multiple views of the process with supportive data – we use a variety of approaches to inform the process	– there is an interlinking of activity and processes	– we record personal and interpersonal data to inform us of the impact of our efforts
clarifying ideas of the process	– it appears isolated and disorganised – we are including a lot of irrelevant information	– different types of information are being shown – we are able to provide detail in relation to some of the general concepts behind the initiative	– we are able to identify patterns and to develop these into action points – we are able to sort details to inform the process – our general concepts are fully supported with specific details	– we are able to show connections between different aspects of the process – core issues are identified and prepared for introduction	– we evaluate the use of the various informative techniques applied during the process to establish points of view and the value of the technique – we generate hypotheses as a result of our actions that we can pursue

Figure 4.9   **Examining the process of change**

	minimal	engaged	active	effective	reflective/ creative
perspectives on the process	– we are looking at this from one perspective only – our perspective is always the same	– we are able to provide alternative forms of presentation of the information we are receiving about the process – we can identify where confusion lies	– we are able to integrate new perspectives to prior knowledge – we are able to identify and resolve misconceptions	– we are able to combine many perspectives in meaningful ways to all concerned _ we can create new applications from our viewpoints	– we show multiple perspectives on our work – we can identify the limitations of our work – we engage in self-assessment of the impact of the process
describing the process	– our present description of the process is simplistic in its understanding of what we are doing / why / and how	– we have a basic grasp of what we are doing / why and how we are doing it – we are attending to the process with our knowledge in mind	– we are actively engaged in thinking about what / how / why things are happening and we are beginning to describe new ideas that are integrated into the present process	– we are engaged in a systematic synthesis of information which we are gaining so that we can then organise core ideas and use them to provide a coherent understanding of our school development	– we are seeking to deepen our understanding of the change process and the school system through our recognition of the many approaches that can be taken in response to improvement initiatives
	1	2	3	4	5

Figure 4.9   *concluded*

Further questions that might be considered are:

- How do you intend to evaluate the impact of the initiative in terms of its effect:
  - on pupils learning?
  - on staff?
  - on the general development of the organisational capacity to adapt to change?

This chapter has sought to show how systems possess powerful drives to maintain stability rather than to change. In order to permeate through the system, it is therefore necessary to understand how they work, and to avoid jumping to conclusions that our responses are going to be correct. In many cases, our actions are temporary rather than conclusive and this is a difficult concept to tackle because it implies that we are always in the process of change.

There are a number of principles which we might work with to assist our approach to the system, and facilitate our understanding of its complex activity.

- Understand and recognise that there will be an underlying structure in existence which will affect what we do, why we do it and how we go about doing it.
- Recognise that all of the parts of the system are going to have connections to other parts, and that although we might be able to see some of those clearly, there will be others which will surprise us.
- Know that a system will resist change in powerful ways and at unexpected times.
- Understand that although every system has its own unique characteristics, there are many aspects of systems which are similar. There are therefore possibilities that we can utilise the knowledge from other systems to develop and support our learning of the one we work in.

5 Learning and leading

We would suggest that one of the most significant roles that schools fulfil is the establishment of capable, competent, self-fulfilled learners. We would also maintain that schools often fail to do this because this capacity is not well embedded in their own staff.

This chapter will therefore address the matter of leading and learning at the personal and the school levels, taking the contemporary theme that such learning needs to be a lifelong process, but also taking issue with the rather narrow definition that seems to prevail over its meaning. We prefer the definition of lifelong learning to be primarily about life enhancement, rather than describing learning as a commodity where another qualification makes it easier to sell one's wares in a competitive market place.

There is obviously an important place for the accreditation of learning and there is a significance to the argument that it is of national relevance to have an educated and knowledgeable workforce. But this diminishes the real meaning of education and is by no means the *raison d'être* of learning. Learning throughout life might better be exemplified as a democratic right and as an ideal expression of personal freedom. It concerns the human passion to discover, to explore, to re-invent and to improve beyond previous personal barriers. Significantly, almost all profound learning involves taking risk, because we move from a sense of certainty in one's view of the world to one of uncertainty, through muddle and confusion into a new clarity.

If we take this approach to lifelong learning and contextualise it within the school setting, there is obviously an important added dimension, namely, that the interest and passion to learn that emerges from the teacher can resonate with students and can in turn enthuse them and initiate their own learning journeys. This implies that we believe that there is a central place for the role of the teacher as learner and leader in the school that is more than the transmitter of the prevailing curricula. The leader in the contemporary school is a moral advocate of learning, and is visible in that role. Whether they then engage with it is a personal choice.

A simple starting point: reflect on the most profound learning experience you can recall, it may or may not be school related. What characterised it? How did you respond? What did you do?

This final chapter is in part a plea that those in positions of responsibility in schools should themselves be advocates of learning. As such, they will stimulate the desire to learn in others, and they will show that the pursuit of learning, and the enjoyment that comes with the discovery and satisfaction of learning, is life enhancing, and that through the enhancement of their learning and leading roles in school they will solve problems personally and collectively.

Learning and the construction of meaning

In the process of working through this book, you will have recognised that the journey towards personal and collective learning often runs counter to that which people are led to believe. Rather than being absolute and pre-ordained, we live in contested times, where the direction that we should take the school system is less certain than ever before. This is despite the rhetorical noises of politicians and policy makers. The certainties of the old system are not working, and renewed pledges to repeat more of the same – 'bigger, noisier, and longer' – will still not make the differences that are needed.

We live in a time of paradox. It is a time where we are witnessing an information explosion, where learning is more often contested than it is shared; it is global as well as local, pluralistic not ethnocentric, dynamic and will challenge the status quo rather than accept it as given. It will pursue dead ends as well as gain profound new ways of seeing issues. It will be mundane as well as poignant.

The development of a 'Learning School' (Clarke, forthcoming) depends upon a wide range of contributing variables. A significant one is the leadership that exists within the school and the ways in which the leaders can 'see' the meaning in the changes taking place in the world around us and can respond sensitively to the demands of that environment. In the development of the role of leader in such a school context, we have indicated that it is important to be aware of the messages that the leadership role portrays through words and deeds. The role will be constantly shaping the ways that people relate to each other, influencing the material that they select to use with students, the interpretation of that material, the way they convey it, and the subsequent meaning that the students derive from it and from the whole process of being a learner inside your school.

An example of the way in which these features of school life are created, and the ways in which a meaning of 'school' is conveyed to all those involved in the community of the school, comes through the development plan. The development plan can be used as a vehicle for rationalising and clarifying the direction and the purpose of particular actions in school. These approaches to the daily work of the school construct a particular set of meanings and establish a mindset that interprets change as planned and programmable. In the short term, this mindset is of use, as it makes the daily routine function. In the long term it is a disaster because it establishes organisational activity which systematises failing practices. The denial of the failure of the approach to change that we seemingly adopt daily as a given, means that the possibility of successful organisational learning is inhibited. Leaders need to develop the viewpoint of the possible, rather than the probable, and accept the notion that they learn from leading.

Some critical questions on leading and learning and learning to lead

By drawing into question some of the assumptions about the 'right' approaches to take to the management of schools, we are suggesting that the successful leaders of the future, be they headteachers or staff members, will have to adopt a mindset that can account for broader features of contemporary school life, in order to solve the challenges that face them, than those which are placed in front of them by policy makers and politicians.

The new leading role

To do this they will have to develop the roles of:

- problem definer – exploring and detecting the meaning in what is happening;
- ideas creator – having the artistry to create new ways of seeing the day-to-day so as to open new doors to learning, and the capability to take the risk to get there;
- evaluator – engineering methods with which to monitor and evaluate the relevance of the responses that are being taken to the problem;

- judge – determining the effect and success of what is done;
- solution implementer – producing a feasible response that will do what is required.

This is not to be done in isolation. It is a collective responsibility, and as such it furthers the idea of 'all leaders, all learners, together'.

Some challenges to our present paradigmatic view

In situations where there is a demand for better than the present level of performance, it is the responsibility of all staff to become leaders and to play an effective role in supporting the improvement of the school.

To achieve this we might advocate progressing along the same developmental routes which have for many years been the mainstream approach to management. These 'scientific' (Morgan, 1986) approaches to management work within the context of linear change where what is done is predictable, and where there are already well established methods of working that are collectively understood and carried out. However, in situations where there is a need to challenge and to change the present way of investigating the way the school is working, the approaches fall short. The following example explores one familiar situation and poses some questions about the way in which such situations might be responded to differently.

A leading problem of change

A primary school spends a considerable amount of time developing a plan for the introduction of change to the teaching of reading. The plan involves all staff, and there is an emphasis placed on the whole-school approach to reading which the school is wishing to promote to staff, parents, pupils and outsiders. Staff attend courses, they have meetings, they review the programmes of study, they purchase different books, they consult parents and they introduce the reading hour with eagerness and enthusiasm.

After a twelve-week period of activity, there is an emergence of unease about the approach. There seem to be teething troubles. Some staff are critical but not willing to openly say so, rather, they begin to modify what they do according to the way that they had gone about teaching reading in the past. They say that the courses are unhelpful, and they feel that their old methods were quite adequate.

The consequence of all of this is that it becomes very difficult to engage in an open discussion on the limitations of the new approach to reading. People seem very defensive. Those that were the key advocates find it hard to admit that the approach has any weaknesses, and suggest that it works in their class so it should work elsewhere. Those who are less convinced demonstrate that pupils are unsettled, and that they find the changes difficult and that as a result it is making too many demands on one-to-one teaching time. The response of senior management is to run a series of further training sessions and to talk about what it will be like when the pupils are more familiar with their new working approach, and to renew the 'reading mission'.

In such a situation, what would you do? We suggest some starting questions here that any leader might usefully reflect upon.

1. Does change like this need to be driven along?
2. Where does change like this come from, and what does it imply of the school's ability to 'hear' its staff?
3. Is it the case that the answer is 'outside' of the school? Do staff always have to be trained, or are there other ways in which the development of the teaching approaches can be managed?
4. Is it necessary to advocate change as something 'new'? The process of re-engineering and pushing away the experience of the past often inhibits the capacity to understand and to respond constructively in the present.
5. Who are the leaders and the followers in this example? What do the relationship of 'leader/follower' imply for the way change might be discussed and explored in school?
6. To what extent was the example one of 'predictable failure'?

Binney and Williams (1995) outline four features of leading and learning which recognise that effective leadership of change involves bringing together what seem to be quite contradictory qualities. They suggest that successful leaders:

- both shape the future and adapt to the world as it is seen,
- know what they want to change and are responsive to others,
- know where they want to go and value the present organisational approaches,
- know what it is successful at and why this is so,
- lead and they learn (ibid., p.52).

Reflect on any one of these qualities. Where might you demonstrate your application of this quality?

The qualities imply that such leaders are able to come to conclusions about the situations in which they find themselves, and are able to hold on to those conclusions and modify them according to their intuitive sense of the present situation and what will and will not be the most likely way to go.

Binney and Williams (ibid.) discuss this ability to live with the paradox of managing in unstable situations in the form of four qualities of leading and learning:

1. the ability to see clearly the shared view of the current approaches that are being taken, and the possible points which can be used as the stimulus for change;
2. they 'work with the grain' making the most of the circumstances that emerge from the day-to-day life of the school;
3. they are able to show how it is a process of 'all' and not 'some' people changing, and that this is personal and related to the school as a community;
4. they learn whilst doing and through doing, creating space as the changes are happening to allow people to reflect and talk about how the organisation is working and why it is doing what it is doing like it is doing.

Using the tension of leading and learning constructively

Leaders have two apparently conflicting stories to examine and to learn from their work in school. They have the day-to-day management of the school as a community which, if successful, will value the traditions and approaches that it has taken to get to where it now stands.

Equally, however, we have a school that will need to be forward looking and to progress. Faced with the need for continual change, the school will need leadership, and this leadership will eventually define itself in the outcome actions which staff decide to undertake. In this situation, attempting to introduce changes through a rationally designed action plan will inevitably lead the school into turbulence and disequilibrium. Because no one has the gift of forward vision, we simply do not know what the future will bring us. This has huge implications for the way we might lead and work with leaders, and think with them about the way in which we approach change in school.

The new challenge – leading in chaos

We know some things about the future which can at least allow us to recognise ways in which we perhaps ought not to operate as leaders: We list a few suggested starters:

The future is unknowable

The long term future of any organisation is unknowable and cannot usefully be predicted.

Shared visions are a myth

If we accept this fact (and unless you are a visionary or a prophet, it is presumably acceptable), a shared vision is going to be an impossible formulation because each person will see different pressures and possibilities. To assume otherwise is to trust in the illusion of the correct interpretation of a past experience which will in itself be of little use to help future interpretation. The same applies to long-term development plans which are developed to achieve such visions. If we decide to use the word vision we must be cautious that this word is understood. We would suggest as one of a whole range of likely challenges that individuals and teams will face, not as something that is static and uncontested.

Searching for significance

Instead, it would probably be far more productive to focus on the ever-developing range of strategic issues that the school is having to deal with. These often come about as a result of ad hoc rather than planned encounters with staff, through casual conversation and informal meeting time. They frequently allow an insight into the things that matter to the staff. They reflect what concerns people and what they feel is likely to be useful for the improvement, however small, of a particular matter that they have expressed concern over.

Seeing clearly

The pace of change in school implies that a school does not locate itself forever to a particular 'vision' because the chances are that this is going to lock them into particular ways of thinking. Rather, seeing the present situation clearly and trying to recognise the diversity of possible viewpoints on the matters of the day will provide more opportunity for growth, and creates a momentum for exploring the meanings of new changes rather than immediately accepting or rejecting them.

Learning cultures are places which contest rather than accept viewpoints

A powerful, unified staff culture can often block the ability of the school to handle changes in the long-term strategic agenda. The promotion of contested, contradictory cultures fostering different ideological perspectives can usefully question the direction and can facilitate the type of learning that is in itself necessary to pass on to learners.

Freedom and control are both important and necessary

There is a paradox between the day-to-day, team management approach that is needed to solve the immediate problems in the school, and the need to establish learning groups of staff where the freedom to innovate and develop new ways of working will create the successful school of the future. Both are necessary, yet many of the present activities which managers are asked to undertake attempt to demystify the nature of the learning and developmental role, and control it and authorise particular ways of operating that are 'acceptable' for the management of the staff culture. This undermines the leadership role in all staff, and reduces it to a series of sterile 'staff development' activities which is often safe, bounded and certain, rather than lively, innovative, irreverent and challenging.

Whilst school hierarchies exist to maintain the status quo, the self-organising potential for teaching staff to function as leaders together is a critical component of the successful role a leader might play because it operates to undermine and challenge that very hierarchy. This is a fascinating tension, it is a vital tension, and it is a necessary tension because without the tension there would be no real change.

Logical and intuitive

Day-to-day working in school must rely on logical processes. But to discover the strategic issues necessary to move the organisation on, it is necessary to develop and heighten intuitive responses.

Day-to-day management requires progress against planned milestones and the continual planning for corrective activity when things go amiss. This type of sustained working which is controlling the development of the school is constrained by rules, systems and rational argument within meetings and official time. However, the control and development of the school into a learning culture is open-ended and is unknowable. The constraints on what is done are governed by staff discussion and by their view of the action they need to take to influence colleagues and to maintain support for the innovation.

Innovations mean risk taking is not an option, it is a requirement

Innovations emerge naturally from the complexity of the mix of challenge and control. Managers who try to control the pace of change by imposing a set of rules will find that these only work in situations where the change is predictable and where there is already a blueprint for action. In many new situations there is no blueprint. This is where the leadership rather than the managerial role is significant because it involves risk taking. The leader will recognise the risk but is willing to assist in the new thinking that is emerging.

Good leaders for the 21st century will drive for conditions in which learners participate in complex, political challenges. These are risky operations, but they are also life enhancing and human activities. They evoke passion and interest, motivation and commitment. The skill is in the ability to recognise the chances and to let others flow into them with you.

Reflect critically upon the ways in which you have recently worked with staff.

- When did you open up the possibilities for innovation, and what were the constraints that you imposed? Try to distinguish between the overt and the covert constraints.
- Why were these constraints considered by you to be necessary?
- What does this imply about your trust in colleagues?
- How could you modify your actions so that more staff were involved as innovators looking forward to a desired way of working rather than responding to the pressures of the moment?
- Is the culture of the school driven? Or is the culture nurtured? What evidence do you have to support your insights?

If you have undertaken some of the activity in this book, you will begin to reconise that the process we are advocating is the development of a learning culture. As a result, there is, in our opinion, no alternative to taking a long view. Short-term quick fixes are fine if you want to continually repeat the same cycles of failed change. Long-term changes in school culture are problematic, challenging and difficult, but they are also powerfully rewarding and worthwhile. To shy away from them is to be afraid to learn, and that is no message to develop inside any organisation, particularly one committed to learning and to the nurturing of learning in others.

Endpiece: Effective learners are effective leaders

This book has raised a series of questions concerning the nature of the leadership role in the post-modern school setting. The implications of this role are that there are a multiplicity of possible directions a school might take in order to achieve its goals and improve its performance. The reality is that many of our schools are located within modernistic approaches to management and development which are fine where there are demands for the school to be stable organisations. However, as soon as there are demands for change, the necessity to take risks and to open up a long-term debate on new ways of working and thinking become paramount. In such situations all previous ways of operating are open to challenge and nothing remains unchangeable. The questions that such thinking raise are troubling because they challenge the way we might believe, feel and wish to work. It does not imply that we have to change, but it does imply that we develop our capacity to understand and to be able to explain more coherently the many changes we put into place.

Whilst this book has indicated that the present formulation of our schools determines that the leadership role is perceived – at least by the general public – as one carried out by the headteacher, we are also eager to show that leadership is now far more than this, and undertaken by many more people. It is an important variable which contributes greatly to the maintenance of organisational effectiveness (Heck and Marcoulides, 1996) but perhaps the most significant aspect of the leadership role is the one which facilitates cultures that in themselves can learn. This within-school culture is something which can be affected by and which in turn affects individuals.

It is time that the leadership role is accepted as a collective responsibility. This brings with it a reformulation of the hierarchical structure of schools which has been inherited from another era when there were simplistic solutions offered to complex problems. We now know that these approaches have not worked, and to maintain the same organisational structure appears bizarre. It is already apparent in many schools that teachers play the leading role in the establishment of the learning culture, and influence greatly the capacity of that school to learn (Clarke, forthcoming). In saying this we endorse the notion that effective learners are the most effective leaders. With the increasing reliance on internal methods of achieving external change, governments and policy makers can ill afford to support efforts to influence systemic thinking on leadership as well as technically addressing present needs.

There are many ways, and we have selected but a few in this book, that leaders can approach the job of changing cultures to address the challenges of their time more appropriately and responsively. This is achieved through addressing what is done, how it is done and through the people who do it. There are observable dimensions of the way many schools are responding to the challenges of leading in the late 20th century.

Other, less visibly tangible, but equally significant aspects of the cultural life and community of the school concern the way people relate to each other, care for each other, and make the effort to appreciate the perspective that their colleagues can offer. School growth and personal growth are therefore profoundly interwoven in a learning and leading process. They are exemplified by the way people feel and go about their daily work.

A leader who can facilitate through action a working climate, who knows the way things get done in a technical sense, who is human in warmth and sensitivity in assisting colleagues to succeed, who seeks excellence in all aspects of the teaching role, who symbolises leadership through their own example as a learner, and contributor to the learning climate of the school – such a leader will establish a learning community in which there is a strong sense of trust in colleagues, an eagerness to promote interdependence in working out problems, in planning both at a strategic and tactical level, in reflecting purposefully, holistically and critically on the intentions of changes, and where risk and stability are accepted concepts in the pursuit of growth of the school. Such will be a leader amongst leaders who learns amongst learners.

Bibliography

Argyris, C. (1990). *Overcoming Organisational Defences: Facilitating Organisational Learning.* Allyn and Bacon, London

Binney, G. and Williams, C. (1995). *Leaning into the future: Changing the way people change organisations.* Brealey, London

Blake, R.G. and Moulton, J.S. (1984). *The new managerial grid.* Gulf Publishing Company, Houston TX

Blase, J. and Anderson, G. (1995). *The micropolitics of educational leadership.* Cassell, London

Bolman, L.G. and Deal T.E. (1991) *Images of leadership.* Occasional paper no. 7. The National Centre for Educational Leadership, Harvard Graduate School of Education

Clarke, P. and Christie, T. (1997). 'Mapping the Process of Change in Primary Schools'. *School Effectiveness and School Improvement*, volume 8, no. 3, pp. 354–368

Clarke, P. (forthcoming). *Living with Complexity: The learning School.* Cassell, London

Clarke, P. and Christie, T. (1996). 'Trialling agreement: A discourse for a change'. *British Journal of Curriculum and Assessment*, volume 6, no. 2, pp. 12–18

Csikszentmihalyi, M. (1992). *Flow: The psychology of happiness.* Rider, London

Danielson, C. (1996). *Enhancing Professional Practice: A framework for teaching.* Association for Supervision and Curriculum Development, Virginia

Fullan, M.G. (1991). *The new meaning of educational change.* Cassell, London

Hargreaves, A. (1994). Changing Teachers, Changing Times: Teachers work and culture in the postmodern age, Cassell, London

Hargreaves, D.H. (1995). 'School Culture, School Effectiveness and School

Improvement'. *School Effectiveness and School Improvement*, volume 6, number 1, pp. 23–46

Heck, R.H. and Marcoulides, G.A. (1996). 'School culture and performance: Testing the invariance of an organisational model'. *School Effectiveness and School Improvement*, volume 7, no. 1, p. 76–95

Department for Education and Employment (1997). *Excellence in Schools*. The Stationery Office, London

Hopkins, D., Ainscow, M. and West, M. (1994). *School Improvement in an Era of Change*. Cassell, London

Loucks, S.F. and Hall, G.E. (1979). *Implementing innovations in schools: a concerns-based approach*. Research and Development Centre for Teacher Education, University of Texas, Austin, TX

Lumsdaine, E. and Lumsdaine, M. (1995). *Creative Problem Solving*. McGraw Hill International Editions, Singapore

Moore, J.R. (1988). 'Guidelines concerning adult learning'. *The Journal of staff development*, 9 (3), pp. 2–5

Morgan, G. (1986). *Images of Organisation*. Sage Publications, London

National Staff Development Council (1995). *Standards for Staff Development*. NSDC, Ohio

Osborn, A. (1963). *Applied imagination – The principles and problems of creative problem solving*. Scribner's, New York

Rosenholtz, S. (1989). *Teachers' Workplace: The social organisation of schools*. Longman, New York

Senge, P.M. (1990). *The Fifth Discipline: The Art and Practice of the Learning Organisation*. Century Business, London

Sergiovanni, T. (1984). *Leadership and Organisational Culture*, University of Illinois Press

Smith, L.M. and Keith, P. (1971). *The anatomy of educational innovation*. John Wiley, New York

Stoll, L. and Clarke, P. (1995). 'Mapping the process of change'. A workshop presented at the National Staff Development Council Annual Congress, December 1995, Chicago

Stoll, L. and Fink, D. (1996). *Changing our schools*. Open University Press, Buckingham

For Product Safety Concerns and Information please contact our EU
representative GPSR@taylorandfrancis.com Taylor & Francis Verlag GmbH,
Kaufingerstraße 24, 80331 München, Germany

Printed and bound by CPI Group (UK) Ltd, Croydon, CR0 4YY

08/05/2025

01864391-0006